Effects of Psychotherapy
With Children
and Adolescents

Developmental Clinical Psychology and Psychiatry Series

Series Editor: Alan E. Kazdin, Yale University

Recent volumes in this series . . .

Effects of Psychotherapy With Children and Adolescents

John R. Weisz
Bahr Weiss

Volume 27.
Developmental Clinical Psychology and Psychiatry

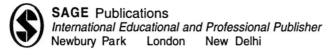

SAGE Publications
International Educational and Professional Publisher
Newbury Park   London   New Delhi

For information address:

 SAGE Publications, Inc.
2455 Teller Road
Newbury Park, California 91320

SAGE Publications Ltd.
6 Bonhill Street
London EC2A 4PU
United Kingdom

SAGE Publications India Pvt. Ltd.
M-32 Market
Greater Kailash I
New Delhi 110 048 India

$R J$
504
$, W 35$
$/ 993$

Printed in the United States of America

Library of Congress Cataloging-in-Publication Data

Weisz, John R.
    Effects of psychotherapy with children and adolescents / John R. Weisz, Bahr Weiss.
        p. cm. — (Developmental clinical psychology and psychiatry, v. 27)
    Includes bibliographical references and index.
    ISBN 0-8039-4388-1 (cl.)—ISBN 0-8039-4389-X (pbk.)
    1. Child psychotherapy—Evaluation. 2. Child psychotherapy—Research. 3. Adolescent psychotherapy—Evaluation. 4. Adolescent psychotherapy—Research. I. Weiss, Bahr. II. Title. III. Series.
    (DNLM: 1. Psychotherapy—in adolescence. 2. Psychotherapy—in infancy & childhood. W1 DE997NC v.27 / WS 350.2 W433e)
RLJ504.W35 1993
618.92'8914—dc20
DNLM/DLC   92-48962

93 94 95 96 10 9 8 7 6 5 4 3 2 1

Sage Production Editor: Diane S. Foster

CONTENTS

SERIES EDITOR'S INTRODUCTION

Interest in child development and adjustment is by no means new. Yet only recently has the study of children benefited from advances in both clinical and scientific research. Advances in the social and biological sciences; the emergence of disciplines and subdisciplines that focus exclusively on childhood and adolescence; and greater appreciation of the impact of such influences as the family, peers, and school have helped accelerate research on developmental psychopathology. Apart from interest in the study of child development and adjustment for its own sake, the need to address clinical problems of adulthood naturally draws one to investigate precursors in childhood and adolescence.

Within a relatively brief period, the study of psychopathology among children and adolescents has proliferated considerably. Several different professional journals, annual book series, and handbooks devoted entirely to the study of children and adolescents and their adjustment document the proliferation of work in the field. Nevertheless there is a paucity of resource material that presents information in an authoritative, systematic, and disseminable fashion. There is a need within the field to convey the latest developments and to represent different disciplines, approaches, and conceptual views to the topics of childhood and adolescent adjustment and maladjustment.

The Sage Series *Developmental Clinical Psychology and Psychiatry* is designed to serve uniquely several needs of the field. The series encompasses individual monographs prepared by experts in the fields of clinical child psychology, child psychiatry, child development, and related disciplines. The primary focus is on *developmental psychopathology,* which refers broadly here to the diagnosis, assessment, treatment, and prevention of problems that arise in the period from infancy through adolescence. A working assumption of the series is that understanding, identifying, and treating problems of youth must draw on multiple disciplines and diverse views within a given discipline.

The task for individual contributors is to present the latest theory and research on various topics including specific types of dysfunction, diagnostic and treatment approaches, and special problem areas that affect adjustment. Core topics within clinical work are addressed by the series. Authors are asked to bridge potential theory, research, and clinical practice and to outline the current status and future direction. The goals of the series and the tasks presented to individual contributors are demanding. We have been extremely fortunate in recruiting leaders in the fields who have been able to translate their recognized scholarship and expertise into highly readable works on contemporary topics.

Psychotherapy for children and adolescents is a topic of keen interest, given the remarkable need for treatment services and the application of alternative therapies to a broad range of psychological dysfunctions and perturbations of adjustment. John R. Weisz and Bahr Weiss provide a meticulous evaluation of child and adolescent therapy. They carefully sift through research and prior analyses of therapy to draw conclusions about who receives treatment, who drops out, the effects of treatment, and the factors that contribute to therapeutic change. From a comprehensive evaluation of the field, the authors raise critical questions about the impact of psychotherapy. Among the special features of this book, *Effects of Pyschotherapy With Children and Adolescents,* are the recommendations for what is needed to move research and practice forward. In brief, the book is likely to be of great interest to those who provide or who study psychotherapy and who wish to understand the effects of treatment.

—*Alan E. Kazdin, PhD*

PREFACE

Each year in the United States, about 2.5 million children and adolescents receive psychotherapy or some related form of mental health care. The national bill for these services totals at least $1.5 billion. Children and adolescents, their parents and teachers, and mental health professionals in many specialties invest massive amounts of time and energy in the psychotherapy process. What is the payoff for these efforts? This book addresses that question.

In this book we try to provide a fair summary of current knowledge about the effects of psychotherapy with children and adolescents. We touch on such questions as which kinds of youngsters stay in therapy and which drop out (Chapter 2), and we explore whether therapy effects differ with child age or gender, with therapist experience, or with variations in therapeutic method (Chapters 3 and 4). But the superordinate concern guiding the book is the broad (and often maligned) question of whether youngsters who receive psychotherapy benefit from the experience.

As we shall see, the answer to this question is quite encouraging, so long as one focuses on the findings of controlled experimental studies of psychotherapy outcome; we review (in Chapters 3 and 4) the findings of major meta-analyses that encompass these studies. However, when the focus shifts to the evidence on therapy effects in the kinds of service-oriented clinics and community-based programs where most real-life child and adolescent psychotherapy actually takes place, the findings are less encouraging (Chapter 5). On the one hand, the evidence on clinic- and community-based care is less than pristine in terms of experimental rigor, and it consequently deserves close, critical scrutiny. On the other hand, it would be a mistake to ignore this evidence and its potential implications.

Accordingly we devote considerable space to a description and examination of the research from clinic and community settings and to a comparison of these findings with the results of more controlled experimental research. From this comparison we conclude (in Chapter 6) that much has been learned but that much remains to be learned about the effects of psychotherapy with young people. What needs to be learned next may well require a partnership between two groups that have operated in relative isolation from one another in years past: experimental psychotherapy researchers and practicing clinicians. It is to the productive interplay of these two groups and to the young people both groups serve that this book is devoted.

We thank Douglas Granger, Wanchai Chaiyasit, Geri Donenberg, Thomas Achenbach, Kimberly Hoagwood, Thomas Lalley, Somsong Suwanlert, Bernadette Walter, Aviva Wasserman, and numerous colleagues in clinics of the West and the East for conversations that have helped shape the ideas in this book. We also thank Julie Mosk for her help in preparation of the manuscript. And finally we thank the many therapists, clinic staff members, outcome researchers, and young people whose participation in research on psychotherapy process and outcome have provided the raw material for this book.

1

SURVEYING THE FIELD: THE PRACTICE AND STUDY OF CHILD PSYCHOTHERAPY

This book is about a type of help that many children and adolescents (herein referred to collectively as *children*) receive every year and that many more children may well need. Reports on the number of children who experience serious mental health problems vary from country to country and from study to study. Within the United States, for example, estimates of the percentage of those under age 18 who meet the diagnostic criteria for a mental disorder range from 8% to 22%, with conservative estimates set at about 12% (Institute of Medicine [IOM], 1989; Saxe, Cross, & Silverman, 1988). This estimate means that, at minimum in any given year, about 7.5 million children in the United States may need help with significant mental health problems.

WHO RECEIVES CHILD PSYCHOTHERAPY?

How many children actually receive psychotherapy in a given year? The Office of Technology Assessment (OTA) (1986) estimated the number of American children and adolescents receiving some form of mental health treatment at 2.5 million, with an additional 5 million in need of treatment. Manderscheid and Sonnenschein (1990), using NIMH data from hospital and mental health officials, generated lower estimates (112,000 inpatients, 552,000 outpatients) for youngsters admitted in 1986. Not included in these estimates or the OTA figures are large numbers of children treated in such settings as schools, physicians'

offices, community centers, social welfare agencies, and juvenile correction facilities. Even those youngsters treated in the more traditional
mental health settings account for a significant percentage of our nation's
mental health bill; in 1986, for example, inpatients under age 18 accounted
for about 12% of all psychiatric hospital days (Manderscheid as cited in
Institute of Medicine, 1989). The annual cost of treatment for disturbed
children is well over $1.5 billion (Institute of Medicine [IOM], 1989). In
addition to this financial cost, families of troubled children often invest
massive amounts of energy (physical and emotional) and time, and mental
health professionals devote entire careers, to the treatment process. How
effective is the therapy provided at such great cost to the youngsters, their
families, the therapists, and society? This book addresses that question.

INPATIENT AND OUTPATIENT CARE FOR CHILDREN

As of 1986 (the most recent year for which we can find statistics),
minors accounted for about 7% of all mental health inpatient admissions
in the United States, with a rate of 177 per 100,000 population, and
minors accounted for 26% of all outpatient admissions, with a rate of
872 per 100,000 (Manderscheid & Sonnenschein, 1990). In that same
year, 1986, outpatient minors were "in treatment" for a median of 138
days, whereas inpatient minors had a median of 25 days (Manderscheid
& Sonnenschein, 1990). These figures bear discussion. The figure for
outpatients refers only to the number of days children were kept on
clinic records; these children actually received treatment only on days
they visited the clinics. In cases where children made weekly clinic
visits, the 138 days on record would translate into about 20 treatment
sessions; however, not all clinics are able to schedule weekly sessions,
and not all children attend faithfully. In a 1990 survey of 1,162 practicing clinicians, Kazdin, Siegel, and Bass (1990) found that the mean
length of treatment reported was 27 weeks, with an average of about
one session per week (this figure may include some inpatient cases). It
is instructive to note that the median of 25 days of inpatient care
reported by Manderscheid and Sonnenschein (1990) represented a significant drop from the median of 54 in 1980 (Milazzo-Sayre, Benson,
Rosenstein, & Manderscheid, 1986). Treatment of children is occurring
increasingly in outpatient settings; mental health workers are increasingly reluctant to remove children from the family and peer group
settings where their real lives are lived. This trend presents a special

challenge to outpatient therapists trying to effect meaningful change in the lives of youngsters whom they may see for an hour or less a week.

Problems for which children are brought to clinics. The children treated in clinics probably represent the full array of syndromes relevant to children and adolescents in the *Diagnostic and Statistical Manual of Mental Disorders, Third Edition,* Revised (DSM-III-R; American Psychiatric Association, 1987), and the *Fourth Edition* (DSM-IV). It is important to note, however, that children are typically referred to clinics not because of a formal diagnosis but because of particular problems that raise concern on the part of parents, teachers, or others in the child's everyday environment—problems such as persistent sadness, explosive behavior, troubled relationships with peers, exposure to such trauma as family violence or sexual abuse, or poor school performance. Many of the most common child problems have been found through principal components analyses (e.g., Achenbach & Edelbrock, 1983) to load on one of two broad-band empirically derived syndromes: *Internalizing* or *overcontrolled* problems, such as sadness, fearfulness, and somaticizing, appear to involve an inward focus and excessive self-control, inhibition, or restraint; *externalizing* or *undercontrolled* problems, such as bragging, fighting, and swearing, appear to involve an outward focus and insufficient self-control, inhibition, or restraint. In the United States, research has shown that the most common referral problems tend to be the undercontrolled variety, but the picture is not the same in all countries. For example, Table 1.1 shows results of a recent survey of outpatient child referral problems in the United States and Thailand (Weisz, Suwanlert, Chaiyasit, & Walter, 1987). As the table shows, all of the 12 most common referral problems in the United States were undercontrolled; the pattern was rather different for Thailand, except that in both countries poor school work was the most common referral complaint.

Of course, the frequency of various child problems in clinic samples reflects not only the degree of concern that the problems stimulate (e.g., in parents and teachers) but also the simple base rate of the problems in the general population. Recent methodological developments (Weisz & Weiss, 1991) make it possible to study the relative power of various problems to stimulate a clinic referral with the population base rate for each problem statistically controlled. This power, or *referability* of a particular problem, is captured in a new statistic called the *referability index* (RI). Table 1.2 shows this statistic for two sets of child problems; on the left are problems very high in RI within the United States, and

TABLE 1.1 Twelve Most Common Referral Problems in Thailand and in the United States

Problem	Type[a]	U.S.(%)	Thai(%)	χ^2	p
United States					
1. Poor school work	U	33.9	35.9	0.4	ns
2. Disobedient at home	U	19.3	6.1	29.5	< .001
3. Temper tantrums, hot temper	U	15.4	11.7	2.2	ns
4. Gets into fights	U	14.3	.8	49.3	< .001
5. Disobedient at school	U	14.1	2.9	30.3	< .001
6. Physically attacks people	U	12.5	7.4	5.4	< .05
7. Lying or cheating	U	11.5	3.5	17.5	< .001
8. Steals outside the home	U	10.4	4.5	9.5	< .005
9. Can't concentrate, pay attention	U	10.2	6.4	3.6	< .10
10. Argues a lot	U	9.9	3.2	13.8	< .001
11. Demands attention	U	8.9	1.1	24.3	< .001
12. Can't sit still, hyperactive	U	8.6	5.6	2.6	ns
Thailand					
1. Poor school work	U	33.9	35.9	0.4	ns
2. Somatic problems (especially headaches) with no known physical cause	O	6.3	29.3	69.3	< .001
3. Absentminded, forgets easily	N	2.6	17.0	44.4	< .001

4

4. Fearful or anxious	O	3.4	12.8	22.6	< .001
5. Lacks motivation to study or learn	N	4.7	12.0	13.2	< .001
6. Sleep problems	O	1.0	11.7	36.5	< .001
7. Underactive, lacks energy	O	.5	11.7	41.6	< .001
8. Temper tantrums, hot temper	U	15.4	11.7	2.2	ns
9. Stubborn, sullen, irritable	M	4.7	9.8	7.5	< .01
10. Nervous movements, twitching	O	2.1	9.0	17.6	< .001
11. Strange behavior[b]	O	1.0	9.0	25.6	< .001
12. Worrying	O	2.6	7.4	9.4	< .005

NOTES: a. Type of problem, as determined by factor analyses of the Child Behavior Checklist (CBCL). U = loads exclusively or predominantly on the undercontrolled syndrome; O = loads exclusively or predominantly on the overcontrolled syndrome; M = loads on both syndromes with about equal frequency across various age × sex groups; N = not included in factor analysis, because it is not listed on CBCL.

b. This category included behavior that seemed odd to parents but that did not fall into any other category. Most was of a type often associated with thought disorder. For example, one child spoke words and sentences that made no sense, and another had a habit of laughing out loud for no apparent reason.

SOURCE: From "Over- and Undercontrolled Referral Problems Among Children and Adolescents From Thailand and the United States: The *Wat* and *Wai* of Cultural Differences" by J. R. Weisz, S. Suwanlert, W. Chaiyasit, and B. R. Walter, 1987, *Journal of Consulting and Clinical Psychology, 59*, 719-726. Copyright © 1987 by the American Psychological Association. Reprinted by permission.

TABLE 1.2   Most and Least Referable Problems in the U.S. Sample, With Referability Index (RI) for Each Problem

| *Most Referable Problems* | | *Least Referable Problems* | |
Problem	*RI*	*Problem*	*RI*
Vandalism	1.13	Bragging	−2.94
Poor school work	0.87	Teases a lot	−2.62
Runs away from home	0.86	Feels must be perfect	−2.58
Truancy	0.83	Self-conscious	−2.55
Sexual problems	0.78	Allergy	−2.39
Steals outside home	0.77	Fears doing bad	−2.25
Attacks people	0.68	Overtired	−2.12
Suicidal talk	0.49	Too concerned about neatness	−2.08
Daytime enuresis	0.46	Likes to be alone	−2.07
Deliberate self-harm	0.46	Obsessions	−2.03
Steals at home	0.32	Prefers older kids	−1.98
Encopresis	0.30	Accident prone	−1.96
Gets into many fights	0.19	Picks nose or skin	−1.95
Destroys others' things	0.14	Lacks guilt	−1.94
Disobeys at school	0.13	Whining	−1.94
Sets fires	0.09	Impulsive	−1.91
Cruel to animals	0.02	Feels unloved	−1.76
Withdrawn	−0.03	Shows off	−1.73
Threatens people	−0.05	Prefers younger kids	−1.69
Lying or cheating	−0.09	Sleeps less than most	−1.67

SOURCE: From "Studying the 'Referability' of Child Clinical Problems" by J. R. Weisz and B. Weiss, 1991, *Journal of Consulting and Clinical Psychology, 59*, 266-273. Copyright © 1991 by the American Psychological Association. Reprinted by permission.

on the right are problems very low in RI. This table, too, shows that those problems most potent in triggering a clinic referral tend to be undercontrolled, often involving danger to self or others.

Independently of referral problems and their referability, one might ask what DSM-type syndromes are most often represented among treated youngsters. In the Kazdin, Siegel, and Bass (1990) survey, practicing psychologists and psychiatrists were asked which syndromes they saw in children they treated. The DSM category most often mentioned was conduct/oppositional disorder; this was followed, in turn, by attention deficit hyperactivity disorder, depression/mood disorder, adjustment disorder, and anxiety disorder. When the clinicians were asked to note the types of problems most often seen independently of DSM categories, they ranked emotional problems as most common, followed by behavioral problems at home, behavioral problems at school, parent-child problems, and learning problems.

Methods of treatment. What therapeutic methods are used to treat these children? Kazdin (1988) identified 230 different forms of therapy that are in use with children. Many of these are used only rarely; however, most child therapists surveyed by Kazdin, et al. (1990) described themselves as eclectic. At a more specific level, the most commonly used theoretical models for therapy were psychodynamic (59% of respondents), behavior modification (55%), and cognitive (49%). When Kazdin et al. asked the therapists to indicate which therapeutic approaches were "effective most or all of the time," they found that individual and family therapy were rated effective by 79% and 59%, respectively. Effectiveness ratings were relatively high for behavior modification (62%), psychodynamic therapy (52%), and cognitive therapy (50%). Of course, it is useful to compare clinicians' views on the efficacy of treatment to the empirical evidence from outcome studies. The reviews and meta-analyses summarized in Chapters 3 and 4 contain such empirical evidence, although that evidence will not be a significant part of what we discuss in this book.

THE LITERATURE ON CHILD PSYCHOTHERAPY, AND THE FOCUS OF THIS BOOK

The literature on child psychotherapy is vast and varied in form. The great bulk of that literature is in the form of case reports—descriptions by therapists of their work with particular children and the outcome of that work. Berta Bornstein's (1949) classic account of her psychoanalytic treatment of a school phobic boy, Frankie, is an excellent example of this genre. Other accounts of child intervention have come from parents, as illustrated by Josh Greenfield's books (1972, 1978) about his autistic son, Noah. Such literature, some published in academic journals (e.g., the Bornstein account), some in the popular press (e.g., the Greenfield books), have helped shape conceptions of child therapy and its efficacy in both the professional and lay communities. In addition, many written accounts describe and sometimes laud the effects of particular methods of child therapy but without supporting data. Kazdin (1988) noted that of the 230-plus different forms of therapy used with children, the great majority have not been evaluated empirically.

Less numerous are published reports of empirical assessments of child therapy and its effects. Some of these are reports of work with single-subject research designs (see Kazdin [1982] and White, Rusch, Kazdin, & Hartmann [1989] for a discussion of such efforts); others employ groups of treated youngsters. In the latter category, we can distinguish among three types of studies: (a) those that include only one group of youngsters, all of whom receive treatment, and that are designed to identify predictors of improvement from pre- to posttreatment (e.g., Weisz, 1986); (b) those that include multiple treatment groups and that are designed to assess the relative efficacy of different forms of therapy (e.g., Kazdin, Bass, Siegel, & Thomas, 1989); and (c) those that include one or more comparisons of treated versus untreated (or minimally treated) youngsters and that are designed to test whether some form of treatment is superior to no treatment (e.g., Stark, Reynolds, & Kaslow, 1987). All three types of group approaches, and single-subject designs as well, can contribute usefully to our base of knowledge, and the three group approaches are sometimes blended within the same research report. For the purposes of this book, however, we will focus only on the third group approach outlined above—comparisons of treated and untreated groups—because our primary objective is to address the question of whether child psychotherapy has positive effects; to answer this question requires treatment-no treatment comparison.

In light of this focus, a number of potentially valuable bodies of research literature will not be covered in this book. As noted above, we will omit discussion of single-subject studies and of therapy research that does not involve treatment-no treatment comparisons. In addition, we will omit treatment-no treatment comparisons in cases where (a) the treatment involved is primarily medical or pharmacological or (b) the intervention is primarily training in academic subjects (e.g., math tutoring to improve grades) or basic self-help skills (e.g., teaching developmentally delayed children to button a shirt). In addition, because our principal focus is on child psychotherapy, we will only briefly note research in which the treatment method of interest is family therapy.

POOLING RESEARCH FINDINGS
ON INDIVIDUAL CHILD PSYCHOTHERAPY:
THE TECHNIQUE OF META-ANALYSIS

For much of the data we survey, we will rely on the technique known as *meta-analysis* (described by Mann, 1990). The technique, introduced to psychologists by Smith and Glass (1977) and Smith, Glass, and Miller (1980), provides a means of pooling and statistically summarizing the results of numerous outcome studies. Prior to development of meta-analysis, reviews of the findings of outcome studies inevitably reflected numerous subjective judgments by those writing the reviews— most important, judgments about what overall conclusions to draw about treatment efficacy. Meta-analysis has at least reduced the extent to which such judgments color conclusions about therapy effects.

Meta-analysis typically involves calculation of an *effect size* (ES) statistic. For each outcome study included in an analysis, the investigator computes posttherapy means on one or more adjustment measures separately for treated groups and untreated (or minimally treated) control groups. The treatment-minus-control mean difference is then divided by some measure of sample variability, sometimes the control group standard deviation, to generate an ES value. A meta-analysis essentially involves computing and then aggregating ES values across a pool of treatment outcome studies.

Like most statistical procedures, meta-analysis has generated controversy. Some researchers have questioned the overall value of the technique, and some have argued that it may generate an inaccurate account of therapy effects. Some researchers, such as Eysenck, have totally rejected the technique, branding it "mega-silliness" (Eysenck, 1978). Others (Mintz, 1983; Strube & Hartmann, 1983; Wilson, 1985; Wilson & Rachman, 1983) have objected to what they view as exaggerated claims made in its behalf or have raised concerns about specific aspects of the technique. In evaluating these criticisms, it is useful to consider Strube, Gardner, and Hartmann's (1985) categorization of the problems associated with meta-analysis. They suggested that the problems fall into one of three categories: (a) those that are potentially present in the conduct of *any* review (e.g., bias by the reviewer in the selection of studies to be reviewed; the editorial bias toward favoring publication of statistically significant findings); (b) those that are a function of the present state of the particular *domain* under review (e.g., an excessive reliance on analog studies; a failure to carefully monitor treatment implementation); and (c) those that are specific to meta-analysis (e.g., nonindependence of effect sizes resulting from multiple effect sizes from a single study).

In a special issue of *Clinical Psychology Review* devoted to meta-analysis, several authors (e.g., Kazdin, 1985; Strube et al., 1985: Wilson, 1985) reviewed the criticisms against meta-analysis. Three of the most

important of these were (a) the inclusion of methodologically weak
studies in meta-analysis data bases has made meta-analytic conclusions
suspect, (b) meta-analysis is a correlational technique with inherent
confounding of independent variables, and (c) the use of multiple effect
sizes from a single study has resulted in nonindependent data points, in
turn resulting in violation of statistical assumptions and invalid statistical tests.

These authors have not been alone in raising concerns regarding the
inclusion of methodologically "deficient" studies in meta-analytic reviews. As Mintz (1983) asked several years previously, why should
anyone bother with studies containing design flaws? If their results
contradict those of well-designed studies, then should not the less well
designed studies be disregarded? If their results agree, what do the less
well designed studies add? However, the number of studies free from
methodological shortcomings is likely to be quite small (Kazdin, 1985;
Weiss & Weisz, 1990) because design compromises, particularly in an
area such as outcome research, appear inevitable (Shapiro & Shapiro,
1983). Even if one were able to find a sample of methodologically
"pure" studies, the sample likely would be too small to allow investigation of correlates of effect size. In addition, it should be noted that
this criticism is not so much a criticism of the technique itself but rather
of how past meta-analyses have been conducted and of the quality of
the literature under review. We address this issue and possible responses
more fully later in Chapters 4 and 5.

The problem of confounded variables is, of course, inherent in all
correlational research designs. Although most outcome studies are
themselves experimental in design, any review must be correlational,
in that the reviewer is not assigning observations (studies) to conditions
(e.g., type of treatment, type of problem). Thus independent variables
such as type of treatment and type of problem may be confounded. For
example, suppose a meta-analysis revealed that systematic desensitization was associated with a relatively large effect size and that, likewise,
canary phobias were associated with large effect sizes. If most systematic desensitizations focused on the treatment of animal phobias, it
would be very difficult to determine whether (a) systematic desensitization was a particularly effective form of treatment, (b) animal phobias
were particularly amenable to treatment, or (c) both a and b were true.
Although clarity may be sharpened somewhat through the use of eliminating or covarying analyses (see, for example, Weisz, Weiss, Alicke,
& Klotz, 1987), the more confounded two variables are, the less,

unfortunately, statistics can do to reduce the murkiness. However, this problem appears to be not so much a function of meta-analysis but of the literature being reviewed. Thus, for this problem (and others), there is little that a reviewer of the literature can do beyond using whatever statistical control is feasible and interpreting findings with appropriate caution. Meta-analysis, given its mathematical underpinnings, lends itself nicely to the use of statistical control. As for caution in interpreting findings, that is the responsibility of any researcher using any technique.

The third criticism, that of nonindependent data points, is more problematic; in fact, we see it as the most difficult issue confronting meta-analysis. Virtually all intervention studies use multiple outcome assessments; thus each study in a meta-analysis (each observation) will produce multiple data points, at least initially. This development violates the general linear models assumption of independent observations, except under the limited circumstances when multivariate techniques can be applied (when all studies being reviewed contain either the same set or a subset of the same outcome measures; Hedges & Olkin, 1985; Raudenbush, Becker, & Kalaian, 1988). A number of approaches to dealing with the problem of nonindependence have been suggested. In their groundbreaking meta-analysis, Smith et al. (1980) used what probably is the simplest response to nonindependence: They essentially ignored it, deciding that utilization of all data was more important than "statistical purity." However, as Glass, McGaw, and Smith (1981) later noted, such an approach can lead to faulty estimates of statistical significance.

There are two other basic approaches to dealing with nonindependence: One may either average effect sizes within each study or treatment group (e.g., Prioleau, Murdock, & Brody, 1983) or select a single ES value from each study for certain analyses (e.g., Casey & Berman, 1985). Unfortunately these approaches all have drawbacks (see Weiss & Weisz, 1990). Averaging can result in lumping potentially irrelevant measures together with relevant measures, and selecting a single ES means intentionally discarding valid data. At present there does not appear to be an ideal solution to this problem; the best solution may be some form of compromise, wherein one averages up to the level of analysis (e.g., Weisz, Weiss, Alicke, & Klotz, 1987).

It is interesting to note that even this concern regarding nonindependence is probably not specific to meta-analysis, in that an author conducting a qualitative literature review is also likely to be influenced by multiple findings from within individual studies. Indeed, the fact that this problem is more apparent in meta-analysis is a function of precisely the characteristic that may make meta-analysis superior to a qualitative review: the explicit manner in which it combines data.

This review of the criticisms of meta-analysis is admittedly brief and certainly not comprehensive; we have left untouched a number of potentially valid criticisms (e.g., nonindependent data points resulting from the same experimenter conducting more than one experiment; Strube & Hartmann, 1983). Our view is that most, if not all, of these criticisms are potentially as applicable to the narrative literature review but that the narrative review suffers from the additional risk of excessive subjectivity. Given a desire to summarize past literature, we believe that meta-analysis is the best approach currently available, so long as it is applied and interpreted thoughtfully and so long as causal conclusions are offered in only preliminary and tentative terms, as should always be the case with correlational findings.

Even among those who accept the utility of meta-analysis there is sharp controversy, much of it over the "best" way to compute and aggregate effect sizes. Each meta-analyst's decisions on such issues are apt to differ in some respects from each other meta-analyst's decisions, simply because so many methodological decisions must be made in the course of one meta-analysis. Space does not permit a detailed discussion here. The interested reader will find ample debate on these issues in the references cited above.

To summarize, we view the technique of meta-analysis, on which much of the material in this book depends, as an important advance but a still-controversial one. Some researchers question the value of the technique, and even those who accept it often disagree about the best way to implement it. Despite the questions and disagreements, we continue to see meta-analysis as a useful way to aggregate and summarize research findings while limiting the potentially biasing effects of reviewers' subjective judgments. Thus much of the material presented in what follows will be based on meta-analytic findings. One final cautionary note should be added: Because different investigators do make different decisions about the specific procedures of their meta-analyses (e.g., different formulas for calculating ES), discrepant findings by various meta-analysts may reflect, to some unknown extent, differences in the methods employed. On the other hand, despite such methodological differences, we will see considerable convergence in the overall mean ES generated by the different meta-analyses of child psychotherapy outcome studies, as reviewed in Chapters 3 and 4.

SUMMARY

In this chapter, we surveyed several issues related to the practice and study of child psychotherapy. We found that about 7.5 million American youngsters have significant mental health problems at any given time and that about 2.5 million receive some form of therapy each year. Children receive inpatient and outpatient therapy for a variety of referral problems. Some of these problems cluster into disorders of the *DSM-III-R* and *DSM-IV* systems, with conduct/oppositional disorder noted especially often among clinic-referred children. Many of the child referral problems also fit within the empirically derived category known as *internalizing* or *overcontrolled,* whereas others fit within the category known as *externalizing* or *undercontrolled.* Methods used to treat referred children are diverse, with more than 200 different forms of therapy in use (Kazdin, 1988). Most of the literature on child therapy is clinical and anecdotal, with only a small portion involving empirical assessments of psychotherapy outcome. However, it is this empirical literature on which most of the book will focus. We will use the valuable, though somewhat controversial, technique known as meta-analysis to review and summarize the literature on psychotherapy outcomes.

2

WHO DROPS OUT AND WHO STAYS IN TREATMENT

To state the obvious, psychotherapy cannot be effective for children who do not receive it. As we noted in the first chapter, many children—perhaps upwards of 5 million per year in the United States—who need help for psychological problems are never taken to a clinic or therapist. In addition to these, many children who begin the process of seeking help, often by going through a clinic admission or intake process, drop out before therapy. Many others begin treatment but terminate before they complete the recommended course. Estimates of attrition from child psychotherapy vary widely but have run as high as 85% (Novick, Benson, & Rembar, 1981).

Attrition is costly both for children and their families and for clinics (Tuma, 1989). For children and families, attrition means that significant problems may go untreated or may be incompletely treated. For the clinic, the investment of staff time in clients who do not complete treatment means that clinic resources, which are limited in most outpatient clinics, are used inefficiently, and premature terminations can have adverse effects on staff morale (Novick, 1980). Because attrition can undermine treatment effectiveness and, more broadly, the work of clinics, research on child mental health care and treatment efficacy needs to include a focus on the process of treatment attrition. This focus can be achieved, in part, by studying the characteristics that differentiate therapy "dropouts" from "completers."

In addition to the limitation that it imposes on treatment delivery, there is a second important reason for studying attrition. As we discuss in Chapter 6, families who drop out before actually receiving treatment represent a potential "no-treatment" comparison group in treatment outcome studies where randomized assignment to an experimentally

14

controlled no-treatment group is not possible (see Weisz, Weiss, & Langmeyer, 1987). Certainly the use of such a comparison group has limitations (Weisz & Weiss, 1989), and at least one key question must be addressed before such a group may be seriously considered: Do therapy dropouts differ from therapy completers along outcome-relevant dimensions (e.g., severity of presenting problem)? If such groups were found not to differ in ways that threaten the validity of the comparison, this would support the use of the dropouts as a no-treatment comparison group.

So far, we have written about attrition as if it were a unitary category—that is, children either complete treatment or they do not. Attrition actually may occur at several different junctures in the treatment process, however, and the factors underlying attrition may vary as a function of the stage in treatment at which the attrition occurs. Building on the phase-of-attrition model proposed by Gould, Shaffer, and Kaplan (1985), we think it is useful to distinguish among at least four types of attrition: (a) *no intake*—children who have an intake appointment but never show up at the clinic; (b) *intake only*—children who participate in an intake but never return to the clinic; (c) *assessment only*—children who participate in an evaluation/assessment phase but do not receive actual treatment (In many clinics, the intake serves as the evaluation, and there is no separate evaluation phase.); and (d) *premature termination*—children who begin treatment but terminate against the recommendation of the clinician.

As we suggested above, the process of treatment attrition can be investigated by assessing whether characteristics differentiate the various dropout groups from therapy "completers." However, these comparisons may be structured in at least two different ways. First, a specific group of dropouts (e.g., no-intake dropouts) may be compared to completers. For instance, Weisz, Weiss, and Langmeyer (1987) compared intake-only dropouts to a group of completers. Second, a group of dropouts may be compared to all clients who progressed past that particular point in the treatment process. McAdoo and Roeske (1973), for example, compared an assessment-only dropout group to a group of premature dropouts and completers—that is, to a group of clients who completed the assessment and began but did not necessarily complete therapy. Both forms of comparison can provide valuable information, although their results may not be directly comparable.

The literature on attrition is extensive enough to have generated several reviews, but the reviews we know of (e.g., Eiduson, 1968) have focused on the problem of attrition across age groups rather than on attrition among children in particular. In one of these reviews, Baekeland and Lundwall (1975) noted that many studies of child attrition failed to find significant differences between dropouts and completers and that, among those who did report differences, many inconsistencies appeared in the findings. Nonetheless Baekeland and Lundwall did conclude that the dropout families tended to have been institutionally referred (e.g., from the child's school) and to be of relatively low SES. In addition, they concluded that the parents of noncompleters tended to deny their child's problems and their own. Not surprisingly, in light of the relatively small number of child studies at their disposal, their conclusions did not distinguish among different forms or phases of dropping out.

In this chapter, we review the evidence we have found involving comparisons of child therapy dropouts and completers. We focus on several sets of variables, including (a) demographic characteristics of the family members, broadly construed (e.g., age of child, SES); (b) child clinical characteristics (e.g., referral problems, severity of disturbance); (c) parent clinical characteristics (e.g., parental psychopathology, parent attitudes toward treatment); and (d) clinic factors (e.g., length of time on waiting list, distance from home to clinic).

SEARCH PROCEDURE, INCLUSION CRITERIA, AND RESULTING POOL OF STUDIES

To identify relevant studies for our review, we first conducted a PSYCHLIT computer search, using *attrition, dropout(s), premature termination,* and *dropping out* as the keywords. These were crossed with *child-* and *adolesce-* to place appropriate age-group restrictions on the search. Abstracts, as well as the title and keywords list, were searched. Then the reference lists of these articles were inspected to identify studies missed by the computer search.

This process produced an initial pool of 36 studies. From this pool we excluded studies that (a) involved mixed samples of children and adults (Morris & Soroker, 1953); (b) involved comparisons between dropout groups and the total clinic population (Lefebvre, Sommerauer, Cohen, Waldron, & Perry, 1983) rather than between dropouts and a defined group of completers; (c) were focused on young people who "dropped out" by running away from residential or inpatient treatment settings (Sledge, Benarroche, & Phillips, 1988); (d) involved telephone interviews assessing the intentions rather than actual behavior of parents on clinic waiting lists (Magder & Werry, 1966); (e) involved comparisons between dropouts and groups of clients who were not offered treatment (e.g., who terminated with the concurrence of the clinic at the end of the intake or diagnostic phase—such as the "pretherapy" group of Cohen & Richardson, 1970); (f) included families who had moved out of town during treatment (Singh, Janes, & Schechtman, 1982); (g) reported comparisons for which the direction of significant effects was not reported or was ambiguous or where the significance or nonsignificance of the effect was unclear (Levitt, 1957a; Lowman, DeLange, Roberts, & Brady, 1984; Sirles, 1990; Williams & Pollack, 1964); (h) failed to identify nonsignificant effects (Beitchman & Dielman, 1983; Cottrell, Hill, Walk, Dearnaley, & Ierotheou, 1988; Ewalt, Cohen, & Harmatz, 1972; Lowman et al., 1984; Novick et al., 1981); or (i) involved comparisons based on procedures that test the unique contribution of each variable to group differences (e.g., discriminant function analysis; Michelson, 1981), because the unique contribution will vary as a function of the different variables in the model. (However, if the article contained sufficient information [e.g., means and standard deviations] to allow us to test non-unique [total] effects, it was included in the review [Lessing, Black, Barbera, & Seibert, 1976].)

We also excluded studies that did not provide statistical tests (e.g., *t* tests) of differences between groups. This limitation characterized a number of the very early studies of attrition from child psychotherapy (e.g., Feldman, 1938). These early studies, several of which were theses for students at the Smith College School of Social Work (e.g., Feldman, 1938; Golden, 1944; Karpe, 1942), generally provided interesting narrative descriptions and tabulations of the reasons parents reported for discontinuing contact with the clinic, but their lack of direct statistical comparisons of dropouts and therapy completers excluded them from our review. After the various inclusion-exclusion rules were applied, a pool of 19 relevant studies remained. These studies are listed in Appendix 2.2, at the end of this chapter.

FINDINGS OF THE REVIEW

Tables 2.1 through 2.4 summarize the results of our review of the 19 studies. Each table contains, in the left column, the identification numbers of those studies that addressed a particular factor (see Appendix 2.1, at the end of the chapter, for the key to these ID numbers). The tables also present summaries of the significant main effects for each factor. Only factors that were addressed in at least two studies are included in the tables.

Demographic factors. Table 2.1 presents a summary of comparisons involving demographic factors in dropout and continuer families. With the partial exception of SES, almost all tests of the relation between demographic factors and dropping out were nonsignificant. Although the majority of studies that assessed the effect of SES did not find a significant effect, four studies found that higher SES families were significantly less likely to drop out than lower SES families, and one study found the reverse effect. Two of the four studies that found a significant negative relation between SES and attrition (Hunt 1962; Lake & Levinger, 1960) involved comparisons of some-treatment (premature terminators and completers) versus no-treatment samples (no-intake, no-treatment, assessment only); thus their findings suggested an SES effect that was felt at the point of the initial decision about whether to begin therapy. However, the other two studies showing SES effects (Kazdin, 1990; Viale-Val, Rosenthal, Curtiss, & Marohn, 1984) involved other kinds of group comparisons and thus were not directly relevant to the issue of beginning therapy. If there were to be a relationship between SES and attrition, the modest findings reviewed here suggest that SES might be somewhat higher in those families who remain in treatment; to the extent that SES is positively related to prognosis, the trend might point toward a somewhat better prognosis in the remainer group than among dropouts, all other things being equal.

Child and parent clinical factors. A number of child and parent clinical characteristics have been investigated, but, as with the demographic factors, almost all tests of these variables have produced nonsignificant and conflicting results. It may not be surprising that child factors are not strongly related to attrition because it is the parent who makes the decision to discontinue treatment (Pekarik & Stephenson, 1988). Thus one might expect that parent factors would be more related to attrition than child factors. As was true for the demographic and child clinical factors, however, analyses of parent variables have produced mostly nonsignificant results. The child and parent findings are summarized in Tables 2.2 and 2.3.

Two studies (Cole & Magnussen, 1967; Gaines & Stedman, 1981) did find that attrition was lower when both parents and/or the entire family

TABLE 2.1 Main Effects for Demographic Factors

Studies	Factor	Number Comparisons	Significant Findings[a]
1,19a,b	Birth order	3	(0)
1,4,5,6,7,10,12,15, 17,18,19a,b	Child age	12	$D > C$ (1)
1,4,5,6,7,10,12,15,19a,b	Child sex	10	(0)
1,5,10,12,15,17,18a,b,c	Ethnic background	9	C:W > NW (2)[b]
1,3,4,5,6,7,8,10,11,12, 15,17,18a,b,c,19a,b	Family SES	17	$C > D$ (4) $D > C$ (1)
1,14,15,19a,b	Size of family	5	$C < D$ (1)

NOTES: a. D = Dropouts, C = Completers.
b. W = White, NW = Nonwhite. Both significant tests for ethnic background came from one study (Viale-Val, Rosenthal, Curtiss, & Marohn, 1984). SES includes tests of the components of SES (e.g., parental income), as well tests of SES itself.

was involved in various phases of treatment. Both of these studies involved comparisons between various dropout groups and completers. Another study (Lake & Levinger, 1960), which involved a comparison of subjects who had received no treatment versus some treatment (premature dropouts and completers, combined), failed to find such a relation, however. As for the two studies that did identify parental involvement as a predictor of staying in treatment, some researchers have suggested that such involvement may reflect parental motivation (Cole & Magnussen, 1967; Gaines & Stedman, 1981). However, three studies (Cohen & Richardson, 1970; Levitt, 1958; Weisz, Weiss, & Langmeyer, 1987) that directly assessed parental motivation failed to find differences between the parents of dropouts and completers.

Some researchers have investigated the related topic of parents' expectations vis-à-vis services at the clinic. Cohen and Richardson (1970) hypothesized that the greater the discrepancy between what families expected from the clinic and what the clinic actually offered, the greater the probability of dropping out. This hypothesis has some support. Lake and Levinger (1960) found that attrition was negatively associated with the degree to which parents agreed with the clinician regarding the nature of their child's problem. Plunkett (1984) found that congruence between parental expectations about the duration of treatment and actual treatment recommendations was associated with lower rates of attrition. It is possible, however, that rather than congruence between the family and the clinic, these findings represent a simple

TABLE 2.2 Main Effects for Child Clinical Factors

Studies	Factor	Number Comparisons	Significant Findings[a]
10,14,17	IQ	3	(0)
	Symptomatology/Referral problems:		
10,12,17,19a,b	Externalizing	5	$D > C$ (1)
12,19a,b	Internalizing	3	(0)
5,10,13	Total	3	(0)
1,2,4,5,6,10,15,18	Presenting problem/ Diagnosis[b]	8	(1)
2,4,14,15,18a,b,c, 19a,b	Previous treatment/ Symptom duration	9	$C > D$ (3) $D > C$ (2)[c]

NOTES: a. D = Dropouts, C = Completers.
b. "Presenting problem" refers to dropout/completer comparisons involving two or more categories of presenting problems or intake diagnoses (e.g., psychotic vs. neurotic vs. character disorder).
c. Three of the five significant effects were from one study (Viale-Val, Rosenthal, Curtiss, & Marohn, 1984).

preference for shorter treatments. Plunkett (1984) hypothesized that higher levels of parental psychological mindedness would be associated with decreased attrition because such parents' expectations would be more congruent with the services offered by the psychodynamically oriented clinic in which the study was conducted; the hypothesis was not supported by the data, however.

Clinic factors. Finally we turn to factors associated with the clinic setting—factors involving such practical matters as the referral pathway into the clinic and ease of access to clinic services. One clinic factor that a number of authors have hypothesized to be related to dropping out is the length of time a family remains on the waiting list. The rationale is simple: The longer the time spent on the waiting list, the more likely it is that the family will become disenchanted with the clinic and lose patience and/or the more likely it is that the child's problems will have improved spontaneously or through help received elsewhere (Lake & Levinger, 1960). In fact, as Table 2.4 shows, two out of five studies found a significant relation between attrition and time spent on the waiting list. However, in both studies the dropouts were on

TABLE 2.3 Main Effects for Parent Clinical Factors

Studies	Factor	Number Comparisons	Significant Findings[a]
1,4,10	Family structure	3	(0)
5,6,8,10,14	Parental symptoms	8	$D > C$ (1)
5,6,8,14,15	Marital status	5	(0)
1,13	Parental motivation	2	(0)
1,10	Stress/life events	2	$D > C$ (1)
2,4,11	Both parents participating in treatment of child	3	$C > D$ (2)

NOTE: a. D = Dropouts, C = Completers.

the waiting for *shorter* periods than the completers. This somewhat counterintuitive finding may be partly a function of the stage of attrition being studied. The two studies that found significant effects (Cole & Magnussen, 1967; Ross & Lacey, 1961) compared premature terminators to completers. Consequently families who were very unwilling to wait would not have been in this sample because they would have dropped out prior to beginning therapy. Time on the waiting list thus may have been an index of persistence, at least in these studies. This possibility might suggest that length of time on the waiting list would have a particularly strong impact early in the treatment process. However, Gaines (1978) failed to find a significant difference between subjects who completed intake and those who did not.

Another variable that has been hypothesized to be related to attrition is the type or source of referral that led the child to the clinic. A number of investigators have suggested that dropping out may be partly a function of the extent to which the parent is genuinely motivated to obtain treatment, which in turn may be related to how coercive the referral is. Gaines (1978), for instance, hypothesized that families who had a "high pressure" referral source (e.g., probation officer) would be more likely to drop out than families who had a "low pressure" source, such as clergy, because the high pressure source would more often be associated with families who were not really interested in obtaining help. As Table 2.4 shows, a third of the studies that assessed this variable found significant results, and, in general, the more coercive a referral source was, the more likely a family was to drop out. This pattern of findings, like the trend with regard to SES, suggests that

TABLE 2.4   Main Effects for Clinic Factors

Studies	Factor	Number Comparisons	Significant Findings[a]
1,3,4,14,19a,b	Distance to clinic/ Transportation difficulties	6	(0)
1,3,4,5,6,11, 14,15,18	Referral source	9	$C{:}NC > C$ (3)[b]
1,2,3,14,17	Time on waiting list	5	$C > D$ (2)

NOTES: a. D = Dropouts, C = Completers.
b. NC = Noncoercive referral source (e.g., self), C = Coercive referral source (e.g., school).

families who drop out may have a somewhat worse prognosis overall than families who stay in treatment, all other things being equal. One might expect that the coercive nature of the referral would have its impact on attrition early in the treatment process. However, no apparent relation was found between the likelihood of a study producing a significant effect and the phase of treatment at which dropping out occurred.

CONCLUSIONS

The most striking pattern across this set of studies is the relative paucity of significant findings and the inconsistent direction of most that were significant. We considered the possibility that the paucity of significant findings was due to low statistical power in the studies. In the studies we reviewed, however, sample sizes ranged from 17 to 539, with a median of 97 and a mean of 146. Thus, with relatively few exceptions, the studies in this review appear to have had sufficient power to detect important differences between dropouts and continuers, had such differences been present.

In most cases where one or two studies produced significant results for a particular factor, as many or more studies produced nonsignificant results. This variability may possibly reflect the operation of unassessed moderating factors. Gould et al. (1985) proposed that the factors underlying attrition may vary as a function of the stage in treatment at which the attrition occurs. Consideration of this factor added relatively little consistency to our findings. Of course, numerous other factors may serve as moderators as well (see, for example, Kazdin, 1990). For example, Gould et al. (1985) found that parental pathology was related to attrition but only among families who received their referral from the child's school. If this were a robust finding, it would mean that two studies testing the effect of parental pathology on attrition might produce different conclusions if the referral patterns for the clinics differed.

Another possible explanation for nonsignificant and inconsistent results is that, for any particular family, any one of a number of different factors may lead to attrition, so no one factor would be consistently responsible for attrition across a group of subjects. The Joneses may drop out because they cannot afford the clinic fees; the Smiths because they did not like the therapist their child was assigned; the Greens because they became frustrated with the long waiting list at the clinic; and the Browns because the stress and complexity of daily living made it difficult to remember and keep appointments. When such diverse factors are combined and averaged within groups, their individual effects may be too weak to produce a significant effect on any one variable for the sample as a whole.

Although most variables that we reviewed produced nonsignificant or inconsistent results, a few factors do warrant further consideration. Four of 17 studies showed dropping out to be associated with lower SES. If reliable and robust, this finding might be explained in several ways. First, SES might function as a marker variable for various resources, with low SES families less likely to have the financial or psychological resources necessary to complete therapy; SES is also linked to such resources as a dependable car and funds for child care while the parents take the young client to the clinic, resources that may be critical determinants of whether a child stays in therapy. Second, it is possible that higher SES families are more psychologically minded and that their expectations about services are more in line with what outpatient mental health clinics offer. In fact, Hunt (1962) suggested that one reason SES may be related to attrition is that the value systems of lower SES clients are less congruent with those of the clinic and the clinic staff.

In this connection, some authors have maintained that when parental expectations are discrepant with the parents' experience at the clinic, the likelihood of dropping out will increase. For instance, Plunkett (1984) found a significant relation between certain expectations and attrition. However, he failed to find a relation between other expectations and attrition. And other findings by other investigators (reviewed above) are not easily encompassed by the matching expectations hypothesis or by a parental motivation hypothesis.

As suggested above, a number of factors may be operating somewhat independently to cause attrition. From the standpoint of the clinic trying to reduce attrition to maximize the effectiveness of its services, this multiplicity is probably an undesirable state of affairs. If dropping out were primarily a matter of discrepant expectations, it might be possible to reduce attrition by preparing clients for their role (see, for example, Bonner & Everett, 1986). However, if only a relatively small portion of attrition were due to this or any other single factor, then intervening effectively would be a challenging task indeed.

As we noted at the beginning of the chapter, a second reason for investigating differences between dropouts and completers is that such differences have implications for the research strategy of using no-intake and no-treatment dropout groups as therapy outcome comparison or "control" groups (see Chapter 5 for examples of studies using such a strategy). The fact that the proportion of significant differences between dropouts and completers overall was quite small supports the validity of these groups as comparison groups.

Even consistent differences between dropouts and completers, however, would not necessarily invalidate the dropouts as a no-treatment comparison group; the import of such differences will depend on their direction. If the pretreatment differences favor the completers (i.e., suggest that the completers have a better prognosis) and if there are no differences in posttreatment outcome between the dropouts and completers, then the pretreatment differences should not be problematic because a lack of posttreatment differences could not be attributed to the dropouts having had a better prognosis than the completers. (Of course, in studies that show more favorable outcomes in continuer groups after treatment than in dropout comparison groups, interpretation would be hampered to the extent that the treatment group had had a more favorable prognosis at the outset; however, as Chapter 5 shows, posttherapy comparisons of treated and dropout groups have generally *not* shown significant group differences in outcome.)

Of the few differences our review found, the majority appeared to favor the completer group—that is, the majority suggested that prognosis was better for therapy completers than for dropouts. For instance, about a quarter of the tests involving SES found that lower SES families were more likely to drop out than higher SES families. One might expect that lower SES would be associated with a worse prognosis, given that it means that the family has fewer resources in general and is likely to be exposed to more stress (e.g., financial problems). The three studies indicating that coercive referral sources were associated with dropping out also support this theme—that is, the findings imply that those who stay in treatment are more likely to have been genuinely motivated than those who drop out.

However, regardless of the direction and consistency (or lack of consistency) of findings in the literature generally, it will continue to be crucial for investigators to compare dropouts and completers in each sample they employ when using dropouts as a no-treatment comparison group because the nonrandom assignment that is inherent in the dropout versus completer design increases the potential for sample-specific differences. In Chapter 5 we present several examples of studies that use this design, with the extent of pretreatment group comparison varying widely from study to study.

SUMMARY

In this chapter we reviewed evidence on attrition from therapy. We searched for demographic factors (e.g., family size and SES), child and parent clinical factors (e.g., child diagnosis, parent symptoms), and clinic factors (e.g., referral source, time on waiting list) that might reliably distinguish dropouts from those who stay in treatment. Overall we found relatively few reliable differences between dropouts and youngsters who complete therapy. A few group differences seemed worthy of follow-up in future research; for example, 4 of 17 studies showed dropping out to be associated with lower SES, and 3 of 9 studies showed that more coercive referral sources (e.g., court or probation officer) were associated with higher dropout rates. The few findings that were replicated at all tended to indicate poorer a priori prognosis for dropout groups than for those who remain in therapy. Taken together, the findings support the outcome research strategy of using therapy dropouts as controls for comparison with treated children when randomly assigned control groups cannot be formed.

APPENDIX 2.1

CODING FOR STUDIES INCLUDED IN THE TABLES

1. Cohen & Richardson (1970). Only the "therapy subgroup" was included in the review because the "pretherapy subgroup" contained individuals for whom treatment was not recommended.
2. Cole & Magnussen (1967).
3. Gaines (1978).
4. Gaines & Stedman (1981).
5. Gould, Shaffer, & Kaplan (1985).
6. Holmes (1983).
7. Hunt (1962).
8. Israel, Silverman, & Solotar (1986).
9. Israel, Silverman, & Solotar (1987).
10. Kazdin (1990).
11. Lake & Levinger (1960).
12. Lessing, Black, Barbera, & Seibert (1976).
13. Levitt (1958).
14. McAdoo & Roeske (1973).
15. Pekarik & Stephenson (1988).
16. Plunkett (1984).
17. Ross & Lacey (1961).
18. Viale-Val, Rosenthal, Curtiss, & Marohn (1984). Viale-Val et al. included no-intake, assessment-only, premature dropouts, and completers. In their analyses, they sometimes performed simultaneous comparisons of the four groups, other times tested individual groups, and occasionally combined

two of the groups for comparisons. For some variables they reported one test; for other variables they reported multiple tests. Thus the actual comparisons that were reported were not consistent across the different factors tested and are difficult to report in tabular format. In the tables, (18) refers to overall tests, (18a) to tests involving the no-intake group, (18b) to tests involving the assessment-only group, and (18c) to tests involving the premature dropouts.

19a. Weisz, Weiss, & Langmeyer (1987).

19b. Weisz, Weiss, & Langmeyer (1989).

APPENDIX 2.2

REFERENCES FOR ARTICLES REVIEWED
IN CHAPTER 2 AND NOTED IN TABLES

Cohen, R. L., & Richardson, C. H. (1970). A retrospective study of case attrition in a child psychiatric clinic. *Social Psychiatry, 5,* 77-83.

Cole, J. K., & Magnussen, M. G. (1967). Family situation factors related to remainers and terminators of treatment. *Psychotherapy: Theory, Research, and Practice, 4,* 107-109.

Gaines, T. (1978). Factors influencing failure to show for a family evaluation. *International Journal of Family Counseling, 6,* 57-61.

Gaines, T., & Stedman, J. M. (1981). Factors associated with dropping out of child and family treatment. *American Journal of Family Therapy, 9,* 45-51.

Gould, M. S., Shaffer, D., & Kaplan, D. (1985). The characteristics of dropouts from a child psychiatry clinic. *Journal of the American Academy of Child Psychiatry, 24,* 316-328.

Holmes, P. (1983). "Dropping out" from an adolescent therapeutic group: A study of factors in the patients and their parents which may influence this process. *Journal of Adolescence, 6,* 333-346.

Hunt, R. G. (1962). Occupational status and the disposition of cases in a child guidance clinic. *International Journal of Social Psychiatry, 8,* 199-210.

Israel, A. C., Silverman, W. K., & Solotar, L. C. (1986). An investigation of family influences on initial weight status, attrition, and treatment outcome in a childhood obesity program. *Behavior Therapy, 17,* 131-143.

Israel, A. C., Silverman, W. K., & Solotar, L. C. (1987). Baseline adherence as a predictor of dropout in a children's weight reduction program. *Journal of Consulting and Clinical Psychology, 55,* 791-793.

Kazdin, A. E. (1990). Premature termination from treatment among children referred for antisocial behavior. *Journal of Child Psychology and Psychiatry, 31,* 415-425.

Lake, M., & Levinger, G. (1960). Continuance beyond application interviews at a child guidance clinic. *Social Casework, 41,* 303-309.

Lessing, E. E., Black, M., Barbera, L., & Seibert, F. (1976). Dimensions of adolescent psychopathology and their prognostic significance for treatment outcome. *Genetic Psychology Monographs, 93,* 155-168.

Levitt, E. E. (1958). A comparative judgmental study of "defection" from treatment at a child guidance clinic. *Journal of Clinical Psychology, 14,* 429-432.

McAdoo, W. G., & Roeske, N. A. (1973). A comparison of defectors and continuers in a child guidance clinic. *Journal of Consulting and Clinical Psychology, 40,* 328-334.

Pekarik, G., & Stephenson, L. A. (1988). Adult and child client differences in therapy dropout research. *Journal of Clinical Child Psychology, 17,* 316-321.

Plunkett, J. W. (1984). Parents' treatment expectations and attrition from a child psychiatric service. *Journal of Clinical Psychology, 40,* 372-377.

Ross, A. O., & Lacey, H. M. (1961). Characteristics of terminators and remainers in child guidance treatment. *Journal of Consulting Psychology, 25,* 420-424.

Viale-Val, G., Rosenthal, R. H., Curtiss, G., & Marohn, R. C. (1984). Dropout from adolescent psychotherapy: A preliminary study. *Journal of the American Academy of Child Psychiatry, 23,* 562-568.

Weisz, J. R., Weiss, B., & Langmeyer, D. (1987). Giving up on child psychotherapy: Who drops out? *Journal of Consulting and Clinical Psychology, 55,* 916-918.

Weisz, J. R., Weiss, B., & Langmeyer, D. (1989). On dropouts and refusers in child psychotherapy. *Journal of Consulting and Clinical Psychology, 57,* 170-171.

3

EFFECTS OF CHILD PSYCHOTHERAPY: I. GENERAL META-ANALYSES OF CONTROLLED, EXPERIMENTAL STUDIES

We now consider the evidence on child therapy effects drawn from controlled psychotherapy outcome studies—that is, studies in which children are randomly assigned to treatment or control conditions. As will be seen, this body of evidence generates an affirmative picture of the efficacy of child psychotherapy.

Because of the large number of controlled outcome studies, some relatively objective method of summarizing their findings is needed. We rely here on the technique known as meta-analysis (described by Mann, 1990; Smith et al., 1980) that was discussed and critiqued in Chapter 1. As we noted there, meta-analysis provides a means of quantitatively aggregating the findings of independent studies, and it permits summary statements of several types about a body of literature, including statements about the average impact of psychotherapy across studies. To our knowledge, four broad-based meta-analyses have been published that have focused exclusively on child and/or adolescent psychotherapy. By *broad-based* we mean analyses in which all methodologically acceptable child/adolescent studies involving comparisons between treated and control groups are eligible for inclusion.[1] In Chapter 4 we survey the findings of more focused meta-analyses and reviews—for example, one that is focused only on studies using cognitive-behavioral interventions (e.g., Durlak, Fuhrman, & Lampman, 1991). In interpreting the results of all the meta-analyses described below, it is useful to keep in mind the guidelines proposed by Cohen (1988); he classified effect sizes of 0.20, 0.50, and 0.80 as small, medium, and large, respectively.

THE CASEY-BERMAN (1985) META-ANALYSIS

In the first of the four broad-based meta-analyses, Casey and Berman (1985) surveyed treatment outcome studies involving children averaging age 12 or younger. Casey and Berman found their studies through a search of *Psychological Abstracts,* through surveys of previous reviews on psychotherapy with children, and through reviews of the reference lists of studies they identified as appropriate for their analysis. The review initially included 75 studies published between 1952 and 1983; however, after some were dropped for various methodological reasons, 64 studies were included in the actual meta-analysis. Studies were excluded if they were directed at purely academic outcomes (e.g., improved math grades), involved only training "to improve or accelerate some aspect of normal psychological functioning" (no examples were given), or relied on drug therapy, peer counseling, or primarily family therapy. Studies involving treatment of parents, however, were included when the child was the primary treatment focus.

Subject sources and target problems. Subjects for the various studies came from several settings and presented rather diverse problems. Some 57% of the studies used school children who had not sought treatment, 15% used community volunteers, 16% outpatients, and 8% inpatients; in 4% of the studies, the source of subjects was not clearly indicated. As for the problems addressed in treatment, 40% of the studies focused on social adjustment difficulties (e.g., aggressive or withdrawn behavior), 13% involved hyperactive or impulsive behavior, 12% involved phobias, and 4% focused on somatic problems such as obesity and enuresis; other studies addressed multiple target problems, thus ruling out classification into a single category.

Treatment methods. Each study examined at least one type of psychotherapy; 19 examined more than one type. Some 56% of the studies included some kind of behavioral intervention. Cognitive-behavioral therapy was the most common of the behavioral methods (used in 21% of the studies), but such techniques as systematic desensitization, modeling, and relaxation training were also well represented. Nonbehavioral interventions were used in 48% of the studies, with client-centered therapy (29%) and psychodynamic therapy (9%) best represented among the nonbehavioral techniques. Some 15% of the studies used therapy approaches so unusual or so vaguely described that they could not be classified.

Effect size computation. Effect sizes were estimated for each study by computing the mean posttherapy treatment group-control group difference and dividing that difference by the pooled within-group *SD*. Here, as in the other meta-analyses reviewed below, a positive ES indicates superiority of the treatment group, and a negative ES indicates superiority of the control group (an adverse effect of treatment). Most studies included multiple outcome measures; in these cases, to avoid certain statistical problems (e.g., inadvertently weighting studies according to their number of outcome measures), Casey and Berman calculated a single ES by averaging effect sizes across all the separate measures. The authors followed a similar procedure for those studies in which multiple treatment methods or multiple control groups (e.g., no treatment, wait list, attention placebo) were compared: An overall mean ES was computed across the different treatment groups and/or the different control groups. (In tests for ES differences between different kinds of outcome measures, however, Casey and Berman selected only one outcome measure per study, rather than averaging.) Thus, regardless of the number of treatment groups, control groups, and outcome measures a particular study employed, Casey and Berman represented that study by a single ES.

Findings. Across the 64 studies that included treatment-control comparisons, there was a reliable advantage for treatment over no treatment. The mean ES of 0.71 indicated that, across outcome measures, the average treated child functioned better after treatment than 76% of control group children. In Figure 3.1, this overall ES is compared with those found in other child meta-analyses.

Interventions involving behavioral methods generated a higher mean ES (1.00) than interventions involving nonbehavioral approaches (0.40), $p < .001$. However, the authors were concerned that studies involving behavioral treatment were more likely to have employed outcome measures that were very similar to activities occurring during treatment; excluding such therapylike outcome measures markedly reduced the ES difference between behavioral (mean ES = 0.55) and nonbehavioral (0.34)

PERCENTILE

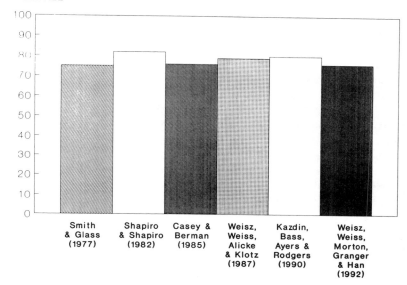

Figure 3.1. Findings of five meta-analyses of psychotherapy outcome research. Numbers on the vertical axis reflect the posttherapy percentile standing of treated groups relative to control groups (the percentage of control group subjects scoring lower than treated subjects, pooling across outcome measures). Smith and Glass (1977) included studies of children, adolescents, and adults; Shapiro and Shapiro (1982) included only studies of adults; the four remaining reports focused exclusively on child and adolescent studies. Note that the Kazdin et al. (1990) bar represents *our* estimate from Kazdin et al.'s (1990) report. Kazdin et al. actually reported separate ESs of 0.88 for 64 treatment vs. no- treatment comparisons and 0.77 for 41 treatment vs. active control group comparisons; we estimate a pooled ES of 0.84, with a pooled percentile of 0.80. Finally note that the bar for Weisz et al. (1992) shows results of a preliminary analysis.

SOURCE: From "The Lab Versus the Clinic: Effects of Child and Adolescent Psychotherapy" by J. R. Weisz, B. Weiss, and G. R. Donenberg, in press, American Psychologist. Copyright © by the American Psychological Association. Reprinted by permission.

methods. (See below a somewhat different method of addressing this issue in Weisz et al. [Weisz, Weiss, Alicke, & Klotz, 1987; Weisz, Weiss, Morton, Granger,& Han, 1992].) Other characteristics of treatment were examined as possible predictors of ES, but most showed no differences. Effect sizes did not differ as a function of whether treatments used play or not, were individually or group administered, or were focused on parents or on children only. Nor did ES differ as a function of therapist experience, education, or gender. Length of treatment did prove to be negatively related to ES. Casey and Berman (1985) thought this might relate to the fact that shorter treatment programs tended to be associated with outcome measures that were similar to the activities of therapy.

The authors also examined ES as a function of various child characteristics. Focusing on target problem, they found lower mean ES for social adjustment problems (0.55) than for impulsivity/hyperactivity (1.10), phobias (1.16), or somatic problems (1.66), with nonsignificant differences among the latter three types. No significant differences were found in mean ES between studies using school children (0.59), outpatients (1.11), inpatients (0.42), or volunteers for special community projects (0.96). Percentage of boys within samples was negatively related to outcome ($r = -.22$, $p < .05$), but child age, intellectual functioning, and school grade were not.

Other ES findings were of primarily methodological interest. Among the various outcome measures, those focused on fear and anxiety (ES = 1.08) and cognitive performance (0.96) generated significantly larger effects than measures of self-concept (0.06) and personality (0.11), but none of these categories differed from measures of global adjustment (0.56), social adjustment (0.48), or achievement (0.35). Outcome measures drawn from observers (1.14), therapists (1.05), parents (0.80), and subject performance (0.74) generated significantly higher ES than measures obtained from teachers (0.19) and child self-report (0.16), but none of these categories was significantly different in mean ES from those measures drawn from expert judges (0.53) or peers (0.47). Importantly ES did not differ as a function of whether the outcome source knew that the child had received treatment. Finally, ES was unrelated to date of publication. On the one hand, this finding provided no support for the possibility that more recent methods are producing more positive therapy effects; on the other hand, it is possible that child psychotherapy is more effective than in the past but that journals are increasingly likely to accept studies reporting null findings, such that each trend offsets the other's impact on overall mean ES across studies.

THE WEISZ, WEISS, ALICKE, AND KLOTZ
(1987) META-ANALYSIS

In the second broad-based meta-analysis (Weisz, Weiss, Alicke, & Klotz, 1987), the two of us joined two of our colleagues in a survey of outcome studies involving youngsters ranging from 4 to 18 years of age. To identify appropriate studies, we used a computer search involving 21 psychotherapy-related key terms (e.g., *psychothera-, reinforce-, therap-, training, treatment*) crossed with age group constraints (*child-, juvenile-, adolescen-, preadolescen-, youth*) and outcome evaluation topic constraints (e.g., *evaluat-, efficacy, comparison*). We also searched the reference lists from meta-analyses by Smith et al. (1980) and Casey and Berman (1985), and we searched *Psychological Abstracts* from January 1970 through September 1985. We included studies conforming to our rather broad definition of *psychotherapy:* "any intervention designed to alleviate psychological distress, reduce maladaptive behavior or enhance adaptive behavior through counseling, structured or unstructured interaction, a training program, or a predetermined treatment plan" (Weisz, Weiss, Alicke, & Klotz, 1987, p. 543). Ruled out were interventions involving drug administration, reading only (bibliotherapy), teaching or tutoring only to increase knowledge of specific school subjects, relocation to a new living setting (e.g., foster care), and preventive efforts directed toward youngsters deemed "at risk." The 105 studies[2] generated by the search process, definition, and inclusion/exclusion rules were published during the years 1958 through 1984. Of the 105 studies, 24 (22%) had been included in Smith et al.'s (1980) primarily adult meta-analysis, and 32 (30%) had been included in Casey and Berman's (1985) child meta-analysis.

Subject sources and target problems. The studies sampled included 163 treatment groups (some studies included more than one treatment). Of these, 126 (77%) involved analog samples drawn from such settings as school classrooms, whereas 37 (23%) involved clinic-referred children. Although a broad range of adjustment problems was included, we excluded studies in which children were treated for mental retardation, insufficient knowledge of a particular school subject, problems involving seizures, and physically disabling handicaps. The target problems that *were* a focus of the analysis were grouped into two categories: (a) *overcontrolled,* sometimes called *internalizing,* problems such as phobias, shyness, and somaticizing, which are thought to represent excessive self-control or inhibition or turning distress inward (see Chapter 1 and also Achenbach & Edelbrock, 1978; Weisz, Suwanlert, et al., 1987); and (b) *undercontrolled,* sometimes called *externalizing,* problems such as bragging, fighting, and impulsivity, which are thought to represent insufficient self-control or inhibition or turning distress outward (see Chapter 1 and also Achenbach & Edelbrock, 1978; Weisz, Suwanlert, et al., 1987). Across the treatment groups of the various studies, 46% involved undercontrolled problems; these were further subdivided into self-control problems such as hyperactivity and impulsivity (19% of the total), delinquency (12%), aggressive or undisciplined behavior (10%), and noncompliance (6%). Another 41% of the treatment groups involved overcontrolled problems; these included both phobias and anxiety (24%) and social withdrawal/isolation (17%). Finally "other" problems not classifiable into either the overcontrolled or undercontrolled category included adjustment/emotional disturbance (6%) and underachievement (6%).

Treatment methods. Across the 163 treatment groups, 126 (77%) involved some sort of behavioral intervention, and 28 (17%) involved a nonbehavioral intervention; the remaining groups were described too vaguely to be coded. Most common among the behavioral procedures were operant behavior modification approaches (24% of all treatment groups), followed by modeling interventions (15%), classical (respondent) conditioning techniques such as desensitization (10%), cognitive or cognitive-behavioral procedures (6%), multiple behavioral methods used concurrently (6%), and social skills training procedures (3%). Among the nonbehavioral methods, client-centered or nondirective psychotherapy was most common (12% of total treatment groups), followed by discussion groups (2%) and insight-oriented, psychodynamic therapy (2%).

Effect size computation. We computed effect sizes in a way different from Casey and Berman's (1985) method. Whereas they had computed a single ES per study regardless of the number of treatment groups, we computed a separate ES for each treatment group-control group comparison (we did not want to risk losing information by collapsing). So, if a study included two treatment conditions (e.g., a desensitization program and a modeling intervention for two separate groups of phobic children), each compared to a control group, we would compute two different effect sizes for that study.

In computing their ES values, Casey and Berman divided the mean posttherapy treatment-control group difference by the pooled *SD* of the combined treatment and control groups; in contrast, we divided the mean treatment-control difference by the *control group SD*. Our rationale was that if psychotherapy leads to an increase in behavioral variability, as some researchers suggest (e.g., Bergin & Lambert, 1978), the pooling procedure used by Casey and Berman (and favored by some experts, such as Hedges, 1982) could cause interpretational and statistical problems (discussed in Smith et al., 1980). In a subsequent analysis (Weiss & Weisz, 1990), we did indeed find that treatment group variability in child outcome studies increased more than control group variability from pre- to posttreatment. In other respects our ES computation methods were similar to those of Casey and Berman (1985); for example, we too collapsed effect sizes across all outcome measures used (except in analyses comparing such measures).

Special data analytic procedures. When investigators conduct meta-analyses, they face a key problem that we discussed in Chapter 1: Across a large pool of outcome studies, important procedural variables (e.g., treatment method and treated problem) tend to be confounded (see Glass & Kliegl, 1983; Mintz, 1983). For example, certain target problems tend to be treated by particular methods (e.g., operant methods for aggression, classical conditioning [e.g., desensitization], and/or modeling for phobias). As another example, age may enter into the confounding because adolescents tend to have problems somewhat different from those of younger children and may tend to be treated with somewhat different methods (e.g., more "talk therapies" with adolescents because of their verbal abilities). Because of such inherent relationships, a comparison of, say, the effect sizes generated by two different forms of therapy is apt also to be a comparison of two rather different sets of target problems and two rather different age groups of treated subjects. To deal with this problem, we carried out planned comparisons with four variables of primary interest: *age group* (children aged 4-12 vs. adolescents aged 13-18), *therapy type* (behavioral vs. nonbehavioral), *target problem type* (overcontrolled vs. undercontrolled), and *therapist training* (trained professional therapists, paraprofessionals [e.g., parents and teachers taught to do behavior modification], and graduate students). We first tested the main effect of each variable on ES. Then we tested each main effect for robustness, using (a) general linear models (GLM) procedures that eliminated (controlled for) effects of the other three factors (see Appelbaum & Cramer, 1974) and (b) tests of whether any main effect was qualified by interactions with any of the other three factors. We applied Bonferroni corrections (Neter & Wasserman, 1974) to other group comparisons to protect against the risk of chance findings.

Findings. Across the 163 treatment-control comparisons, we found a mean ES of 0.79. Across the various outcome measures used in the various studies, the average treated youngster after treatment scored at the 79th percentile of the control group youth. Only 6% of the treatment-control comparisons yielded negative effect sizes, a result that indicates adverse effects of treatment. These overall ES findings were similar to those of Casey and Berman (1985; see Figure 3.1).

Next we compared the effect sizes generated by behavioral methods (126 treatment-control comparisons) versus nonbehavioral (27 comparisons); the behavioral ES was significantly higher (means: 0.88 vs. 0.44; $p > .05$). The difference remained significant when we used eliminating tests to control for age, for problem type, and for therapist training; moreover, interactions of therapy type with problem type and with therapist training were not significant.

Following Casey and Berman (1985), we further examined the therapy type effect by excluding comparisons in which outcome measures were similar to treatment procedures. This process eliminated 63% of the studies and reduced the behavioral-nonbehavioral difference to nonsignificance. However, we were concerned that the Casey-Berman procedure might rule out many well-designed studies in which outcome measures similar to training procedures are appropriate and necessary for a fair test of therapy effects. For example, when children are treated for fear of animals or the dark through modeling or reinforcement of approach behavior, the most fitting outcome measure may be the children's approach behavior, despite its similarity to the treatment activity. In other studies the use of outcome measures that are similar to treatment methods is clearly not necessary. For example, when the Matching Familiar Figures Test is used to teach reflective behavior to children who have attentional problems, the same test need not be used to measure outcomes because the goal of treatment is broader than improved performance on this particular test. Following this reasoning, we distinguished between studies in which similarity of outcome measures and treatment procedures was necessary for a fair test and studies in which such similarity was unnecessary. When we reinstated the former studies and recomputed the behavioral versus nonbehavioral comparison, we again found higher ES for behavioral than for non-behavioral methods ($p < .05$; means: 0.93 vs. 0.45).

Beyond the overall behavioral-nonbehavioral comparison, we found no significant ES difference between more specific behavioral methods (e.g., operant vs. modeling) or nonbehavioral methods (e.g., insight-oriented psychodynamic vs. client-centered); however, comparisons of nonbehavioral methods were hard to interpret clearly because 20 of the 27 nonbehavioral interventions involved client-centered therapy. Only three studies involved insight-oriented psychodynamic therapy, the most widely used method in clinical practice (see Kazdin, Siegel, & Bass, 1990); the mean ES across these three studies was 0.01, indicating no significant treatment effect. Clearly we need a richer base of evidence on this widely practiced form of intervention.

When we focused on child characteristics, we found no reliable difference in mean ES between studies treating mostly girls (ES = 1.11) and studies treating mostly boys (0.80); by contrast, Casey and Berman (1985) found higher ES values for girls than boys. Unlike Casey and Berman, we found an age main effect: The 98 treatment-control comparisons involving children (aged 4-12) generated a higher mean ES than the 61 comparisons involving adolescents (aged 13-18) (means: 0.92, 0.58; $p < .05$). The correlation between age and ES was -0.21 ($p < .05$) over the entire sample. The magnitude of the age effect was reduced slightly when therapy type (behavioral vs. nonbehavioral) was controlled and when problem type (over- vs. undercontrolled) was controlled, but the age group effect grew stronger when therapist training was controlled.

Age did not interact significantly with therapy type or problem type, but we did find a significant age × therapist training interaction ($p < .05$): Age and ES were uncorrelated among professional therapists ($r = .11$) but were significantly correlated among graduate students ($r = -.31, p < .05$) and paraprofessionals ($r = -.43, p < .05$). In essence, professional therapists were about equally effective with all ages, but graduate students and paraprofessionals were more effective with younger than with older clients.

Focusing next on the target problems for which youngsters were treated, we found no significant mean ES difference between the broad categories of overcontrolled and undercontrolled problems. This null finding held when we used eliminating tests to control for age level, therapy type, and therapist training. On the other hand, when we tested interactions involving problem type, we did find a marginal interaction with therapist training ($p = .059$). The three therapist types did not differ in their mean ES with undercontrolled problems; however, with over-controlled problems, mean ES did increase with increases in professional training from paraprofessional (mean ES: 0.53) to graduate student (0.71) to professional therapist (1.03). The pattern suggests the possibility that advanced training and experience make a bigger difference with overcontrolled or internalizing problems than with undercontrolled problems.

Casey and Berman (1985) found significant differences in ES as a function of the content and source of the outcome measures. We found reliable differences only for the source of outcome measures. Measures taken from trained observers (mean ES 1.08) showed a significantly larger ES than did measures taken from parents (0.66), teachers (0.68), subject performance (0.65), subject report (0.49), or peer report (0.33; all ps < .05); no reliable difference was found among the latter five sources.

We also found a higher mean ES for youngsters treated individually (1.04) than for those treated in groups (means: 1.04 vs. 0.62, $p < .05$), but the difference was not significant after Bonferroni correction. In addition, we found that mean ES measured immediately after the conclusion of treatment was not reliably different from mean ES at later follow-up assessments (averaging 168 days after treatment termination). And we found that the mean ES of comparisons using clinic-referred children was not reliably different from the mean ES of studies using *analog samples,* that is, children recruited (e.g., from schools) by researchers for their treatment studies. This finding is potentially important because outcome research has been criticized in the past for reliance on analog samples rather than on true clinic cases (see, for example, Parloff, 1984; Shapiro & Shapiro, 1982).

THE KAZDIN, BASS, AYERS, AND RODGERS
(1990) META-ANALYSIS

The third meta-analysis we will describe was presented as one part of a broader survey by Kazdin, Bass, Ayers, and Rodgers (1990) of the characteristics of research on child psychotherapy. The studies that were surveyed involved youngsters in the age range of 4 to 18. The initial pool included 223 studies that had been published between 1970 and 1988, but the meta-analysis involved a smaller subset: A total of 105 of the studies were actually used to compute ES data for treatment versus control group comparisons. Of these 105 studies, our calculations indicated that 13% had also been used in the Casey-Berman (1985) meta-analysis, and 18% had been used in the Weisz, Weiss, Alicke, and Klotz (1987) meta-analysis. The initial search for studies was based on a definition of *psychotherapy* as "an intervention designed to decrease distress, symptoms, and maladaptive behavior and/or to improve adaptive and prosocial functioning" (Kazdin, Bass, et al., 1990, p. 730). Kazdin, Bass, et al. required that the intervention include "some form of counseling, structured or unstructured interaction, training program, or plan" or that it draw "upon psychosocial influences such as discussion, learning, persuasion that focuses on how clients feel (affect), think (cognition), or act (behavior)" (p. 730). Excluded were interventions involving medication and those aimed only at "educational, career, or vocational goals" (p. 730). Computer search terms were drawn from previous meta-analyses (e.g., Casey & Berman, 1985; Weisz, Weiss, Alicke, & Klotz, 1987) and from previous surveys of clinical practice (e.g., Tuma & Pratt, 1982).

Subjects and their target problems. Over the full sample of 223 studies, the mean age of treated children was 10.2 years, with 75% of the studies in the 6 to 11-year age range. Some 67% of the cases were boys. Only 20% of the studies specified the race or ethnic group of their subjects; white, black, and Latino youth were included in 76%, 66%, and 18% of these studies, respectively. As for the source of subjects, 77% used analog cases recruited by the researchers, 28% used clinic referred, 3% inpatients, 1% court referred, and 1% incarcerated. When problems were classified into general categories, 51% of the studies involved children treated for acting-out behavior, 22% for behavior problems at home, 20% for learning problems, 19% for emotional problems, and 10% for behavior problems at school. Using an alternate category scheme, Kazdin et al. found that 47% of the studies involved children treated for externalizing problems, 16% for internalizing, 3% for both internalizing and externalizing, and 15% for learning/academic problems.

Treatment methods. Kazdin et al. also classified treatment methods used in the studies. Behavior modification was used in 50% of the studies, cognitive-behavioral approaches in 22%, group therapy in 9%, client-centered therapy in 5%, play therapy in 5%, family therapy in 4%, and various other approaches in fewer than 4% of the studies.

Effect size computation. Effect sizes were calculated following procedures very similar to those used by Casey and Berman (1985), with the mean posttherapy treatment group-control group difference divided by the pooled within-group *SD*. For each study an ES was computed for each pair of groups compared, and group comparisons were classified into three categories: treatment versus no-treatment, treatment versus active control group, and treatment versus treatment (i.e., comparison of different treatment approaches). For our purposes the first two categories are of interest.

Findings. For the 64 studies involving treatment versus no-treatment comparisons, Kazdin et al. found a mean ES of 0.88; this finding indicates that the average treated child after treatment was at the 81st percentile of the no-treatment group, pooling across outcome measures. For the 41 studies involving treatment versus active control comparisons, the mean ES was 0.77, indicating that the average treated child after treatment was at the 78th percentile of the control group. For those 41% of the studies that included follow-up assessments (median duration of the longest follow-up period: 5 months), Kazdin et al. reported ES at follow-up: 0.89 for treatment-no treatment comparisons, 0.39 for treatment-active control comparisons. Thus treatment gains held steady for treatment-no treatment comparisons but not so steady for comparisons involving active control conditions.

It was not the purpose of Kazdin et al. to compare the relative efficacy of different therapy approaches. Nor did they attempt to assess relations between ES and target problem, child characteristics, therapist characteristics, or type or source of outcome measure. They did, however, assess mean ES for comparisons of one treatment versus another treatment (e.g., operant vs. modeling). The mean ES, based on absolute differences between effects of the contrasting treatments, was 0.59, with a mean ES at follow-up of 0.64. Thus the immediate posttherapy ESs for treatment versus no-treatment comparisons (0.88) and treatment versus active control comparisons (0.77) were in the range of *large* effects, following Cohen (1988), whereas the ES for treatment versus treatment comparisons was in the *medium* range.

THE WEISZ, WEISS, MORTON, GRANGER, AND HAN (1992) META-ANALYSIS

The fourth and final meta-analysis we describe in this chapter is another in which we joined forces with colleagues (Weisz, Weiss, Morton, Granger, & Han, 1992). We are still in the final stages of data analysis, so the report we give in this chapter must be considered preliminary. In this new meta-analysis, we surveyed all the studies we could find that had not been included in the Casey and Berman (1985) meta-analysis or the Weisz, Weiss, Alicke, and Klotz (1987) meta-analysis. (We did not exclude studies included in the Kazdin, Bass, et al. [1990] survey and meta-analysis because we wanted to include tests of the impact of such factors as treatment method, treated problem, and therapist experience—tests that were not a focus of the Kazdin et al. report.) To identify relevant studies, we used several steps. We conducted a computer search for the years 1983 through 1991, employing the same 21 psychotherapy-related key terms used in Weisz, Weiss, Alicke, and Klotz (1987; see above), crossed with the same age group constraints and outcome-assessment constraints used in that meta-analysis. Still focusing on the 1983 through 1991 time period, we also searched by hand, issue by issue, those journals that had produced articles in our 1987 meta-analysis. As a third step, we searched the reference lists of all the articles we found that met our inclusion criteria. Finally we reviewed the list of studies included in previous meta-analyses by Smith et al. (1980) and Kazdin, Bass, et al. (1990) to identify any articles that fit our criteria and that might have been missed in the other three steps of our search. This process produced a pool of 110 studies (plus two others that included only follow-up reports).

The studies had been published between 1967 and 1991. Across the 110 studies the mean age of the children ranged from 1.5 to 17.6 years. Because the idea of "child psychotherapy" with 1½-year-old children may sound implausible, we should note that studies focusing on very young children involved parent-training interventions.

Subject sources and target problems. The studies sampled included 178 treatment groups; 99 (56%) involved youngsters who had been referred for treatment, and 77 (43%) involved children selected for treatment by the research project (2 treatment groups were not codable on this dimension). As in our 1987 meta-analysis, we included children being treated for a broad range of emotional and behavioral problems, but we excluded studies focusing on the treatment of mental retardation, insufficient knowledge of a particular school subject, and problems involving physical disabilities. Target problems again were classified as (a) overcontrolled (e.g., phobias, depression), (b) undercontrolled (e.g., aggression), or (c) other (e.g., autism, impaired social relations). Of the 178 treatment groups, 40.3% focused on the treatment of undercontrolled problems; these were further subdivided into delinquency (8% of the total), noncompliance (2%), self-control problems such as hyperactivity and impulsivity (12%), aggression (8%), and mixed undercontrolled problems (11%). Another 30.3% of the treatments focused on overcontrolled problems, these were further subdivided into phobias and anxiety (10%), social withdrawal (2%), depression (4%), and somatic problems (e.g., headaches, 13%). Finally, 29.4% of the treatment groups focused on other problems, which included mixed over- and undercontrolled problems (15%), impaired social relations (9%), underachievement (1%), personality problems (3%), and problems not otherwise categorized (e.g., autism, 2%).

Treatment methods. Of the 178 treatment groups, 151 (85%) involved some form of behavioral treatment, and 20 (11%) involved nonbehavioral treatments (in our 1987 sample, 77% were behavioral, 17% nonbehavioral); the remaining studies either involved both techniques or were too vaguely described to be coded. In our 1987 meta-analysis the most common behavioral treatment approach was operant (24% of total); however, in the 1992 sample the most common form of behavioral treatment was cognitive/cognitive-behavioral (17% of total). Treatment groups using operant techniques comprised 10% of the sample, respondent techniques 14%, modeling 7%, social skills training 6%, and parent training 14%. Among the nonbehavioral methods, client-centered or nondirective psychotherapy accounted for 2% of the total sample; general discussion groups 4%; and insight-oriented, psychodynamic treatment 5%.

Effect size computation. As in our 1987 meta-analysis, we divided treatment group-control group differences by the *SD* of the control group because evidence (Weiss & Weisz, 1990) suggests that treatment groups and control groups differ significantly on outcome measure variability at posttreatment. The present analysis did differ from the

1987 analysis, however, in that we consistently collapsed across outcome measures up to the level of analysis. Thus, for instance, in the analysis of source of outcome measure, each study produced one ES per category within source. (To compare our 1992 results to our 1987 results, however, we also performed the analyses not collapsing across outcome measures when assessing the outcome measure characteristics. Results were essentially the same for both methods.)

Findings. Across the 110 studies, the mean posttreatment ES was 0.71, which differed significantly from zero (p < .0001). The average treated child scored at the 76th percentile of the control group children. This ES is identical to that reported by Casey and Berman (1985) and is similar to the values reported by Weisz, Weiss, Alicke, and Klotz (1987) and Kazdin, Bass, et al. (1990). Eight percent of the studies had an overall negative ES, indicating that only a small minority of treatments had an adverse effect.

We next compared the ES for behavioral treatments to that for nonbehavioral methods. ES averaged 0.80 for behavioral interventions, 0.32 for nonbehavioral. Because the ES variance was significantly greater for the behavioral groups than for nonbehavioral groups (behavioral = 12 × nonbehavioral partly because ES for nonbehavioral groups was so uniformly low), we used a nonparametric analysis to compare the two ES means. The Wilcoxon 2-sample test indicated that the two groups differed significantly (p < .03). When we excluded from the analysis outcome the measures that were unnecessarily similar to the treatment (see our discussion of this issue on p. 32, 38-39), the test remained significant (p < .01). Thus, as we found in our 1987 meta-analysis, behavioral treatments showed a stronger ES than nonbehavioral, and the difference did not appear to be a function of unnecessary overlap between the treatment methods and outcome measures.

We tested other effects that had been examined in our 1987 sample of studies (Weisz, Weiss, Alicke, & Klotz, 1987). We found a significant correlation ($r = -.23$, $p < .05$) between the percentage of boys in a sample and the ES, indicating that the greater the proportion of boys in the sample, the worse the outcome of treatment; this finding is consistent with the findings of Casey and Berman (1985) but inconsistent with our 1987 findings, which showed no significant relation between ES and gender of treated youngsters.

Beyond the gender effect, we found no other significant main effects. Tests for effects of subject age (linear and quadratic terms, as well as a categorical variable), target problem (overcontrolled vs. undercontrolled), outcome measure domain (overcontrolled vs. undercontrolled), source of outcome measure (coded as in Weisz, Weiss, Alicke, & Klotz, 1987), group versus individual treatment, type of control group (assessment only, waiting list, attention placebo, minimal treatment), therapist training (coded as in Weisz, Weiss, Alicke, & Klotz, 1987), analog versus referred sample, sample size, year of publication, and posttreatment versus follow-up were all nonsignificant.

We also tested the two-way interactions among our four main variables (age, type of treatment, type of problem, therapist training). The interaction between age and therapist training was significant, $F(2,121) = 6.46$, $p < .005$. As in our 1987 meta-analysis, the effect of age was nonsignificant for the professionals but was significant for paraprofessionals and for students. However, although the paraprofessionals were again more effective with younger than with older children ($r = -.40$), in the present sample the students were more effective with older than with younger children ($r = .31$), in contrast to our 1987 findings. No other interactions were significant.

SUMMARIZING FINDINGS
OF THE FOUR BROAD-BASED META-ANALYSES

The characteristics and findings of the four broad-based meta-analyses are summarized in Table 3.1. We also note whether the ES calculation involved dividing by the *SD* of the control group only or by the pooled *SD* of both groups being compared. Figure 3.1 provides a graphic comparison of the findings of the four child meta-analyses plus the findings of two widely cited meta-analyses of predominantly adult psychotherapy studies (Shapiro & Shapiro, 1982; Smith et al., 1980). The comparison indicates that the mean effect sizes reported in child meta-analyses are quite comparable to those of adult meta-analyses and that findings in both categories point to quite positive effects of therapy. Mean ESs for comparisons made immediately after therapy range from 0.71 to 0.80; as noted earlier, Cohen (1988) classified effect sizes as small, medium, and large, respectively, if they reach 0.20, 0.50, and 0.80, respectively. In addition, the mean follow-up ES figures, shown in Table 3.1, suggest that the therapy effects have reasonable staying power. We must qualify this statement by noting that in each of the four meta-analyses the percentage of the original pool of studies for which

TABLE 3.1 Overview of the Broad-Based Meta-Analyses

	Casey & Berman (1985)	*Weisz, Weiss, Alicke, & Klotz (1987)*	*Kazdin, Bass, Avery & Rodgers (1990)*[a]	*Weisz, Weiss, Morton, Granger, & Han (1992)*
Number of studies	64	105	64/41	110
Mean age across studies	8.9	10.2	10.2	10.3
Age range (study means)	3-12	4-18	5-18	2-18
Percentage male subjects	60	66	67	63
Effect Size (ES) Findings:				
Mean posttherapy ES	.71	.79	.88/.77	.71
Percentile of treated Ss	76	79	81/78	76
Mean follow-up ES	.60	.93	.89/.39	.61
Behavioral >				
Nonbehavioral?	yes/no	yes	NE	yes
Females > Males?	yes	no	NE	yes
Younger > Older Ss?	no	yes	NE	no
Recent > Older studies?	no	NE	NE	no
Over- > Undercontrolled?	NE	no	NE	no
ES formula used	$\dfrac{M1 - M2}{SD \text{ (pooled)}}$	$\dfrac{M1 - M2}{SD \text{ (controls)}}$	$\dfrac{M1 - M2}{SD \text{ (pooled)}}$	$\dfrac{M1 - M2}{SD \text{ (controls)}}$

NOTE: a. The Kazdin, Bass, et al. (1990) study began with a sample of 223 studies, but many of these did not contain a treatment vs. control group comparison; the meta-analysis was applied separately to those studies involving treatment vs. no-treatment comparisons ($N = 64$ studies) and those studies involving treatment vs. active control group comparisons ($N = 41$ studies). In the Kazdin, Bass, et al. column of the table, wherever we list one figure only, we are referring to the original sample of 223 studies; wherever we list two figures separated by a slash (/), we are referring to the two separate meta-analytic calculations.
NE = Not examined in this meta-analysis.

follow-up assessments were made was relatively small and that the average length of the period between end of therapy and follow-up assessment tended to be less than 6 months.

TWO LIMITATIONS
OF THE META-ANALYTIC DATA

Because the four meta-analyses reflect such a large number of distinct outcome studies ($N > 200$) and subjects ($N > 11,000$), it may be tempting to conclude that the evidence on child therapy effects is now in and that the pattern of findings is rather clear. Such a conclusion may be premature, however. One obvious reason is that the findings of the various meta-analyses do not converge in every respect (e.g., whether effect sizes tend to be larger for girls than boys). Moreover, although meta-analysis is certainly useful as a way of reducing subjectivity when summarizing research findings, it is important to note certain limitations in the meta-analytic data reviewed here. These limitations cloud interpretation of the evidence on predictors of ES and on overall ES.

Evidence on correlates of effect size is clouded by confounding of factors. It is difficult through meta-analysis to generate clear, unambiguously interpretable data on possible correlates of ES—for example, therapy methods, target problems, and child age and gender because such factors are inherently confounded to some degree in any large sample of child therapy studies. We discussed this issue earlier in this chapter and in Chapter 1. This confounding can be addressed, in part, through procedures such as the eliminating and interaction tests employed by Weisz et al. (Weisz, Weiss, Alicke, & Klotz, 1987; Weisz et al., 1992); however, such tests cannot fully correct for all the confounding that is inevitably present. The best way to address this problem is to pool multiple studies in which the comparisons of interest have been made with matched samples—for example, studies in which behavioral and nonbehavioral treatment methods have been used with separate demographically and clinically matched samples. At this point, however, the array of outcome studies available would not permit sufficient pooling to address more than a limited number of very focused questions. With time, as the pool of outcome studies is enriched, more matched comparisons will be possible.

Evidence on the overall (mean) effect of therapy is clouded by the unrepresentativeness of most studies. A second limitation of the evidence makes it difficult to know how much we can generalize from the positive overall ES found in the four meta-analyses. Most of the outcome studies included in the meta-analyses appear to have involved children, interventions, and/or treatment conditions that are relatively unrepresentative of conventional clinical practice. As noted by Weisz and Weiss (1989), in many of these controlled experimental studies, (a) youngsters were recruited for treatment, not actually clinic referred, which suggests that they were not seriously disturbed; (b) samples were selected for homogeneity, with all youngsters displaying a similar focal problem or problems (e.g., a specific phobia or out-of-seat behavior in school); (c) therapy addressed the focal problem(s) primarily or exclusively; (d) therapists were trained immediately prior to therapy in the specific techniques they would use; and (e) the therapy involved primary or exclusive reliance on those techniques. Kazdin, Bass, et al. (1990) detailed and documented a number of important differences between the circumstances arranged for most outcome research and the conditions prevailing in most clinical practice. In Chapter 5 we discuss these differences and turn our attention to an important question suggested by these differences: Are the benefits of therapy as demonstrated in controlled outcome studies matched by the benefits of actual clinical practice with children?

Before addressing this question, however, we round out the picture of psychotherapy effects in controlled experimental studies. We do this in Chapter 4 by surveying more narrowly focused meta-analyses and reviews on specific types of therapy and specific questions about therapy effects.

SUMMARY

In this chapter we surveyed experimental literature on the effects of child psychotherapy. We focused on the evidence from four broad, general meta-analyses encompassing well over 200 controlled studies. Overall, the evidence showed positive effects of therapy, effects approaching a level that Cohen's (1988) classification scheme would categorize as large. All four meta-analyses found mean effect sizes higher than 0.70, with the average treated child scoring higher after treatment than more than three quarters of control group children on a variety of outcome measures. Some evidence was found that behavioral therapies yielded stronger effects than nonbehavioral approaches and that girls showed more positive effects than boys, but neither finding was consistent across all the meta-analyses. Finally, we noted two limitations of the meta-analytic evidence: (a) The confounding of factors (e.g., treated problem and type of treatment) makes it difficult to interpret evidence on the correlates of effect size (e.g., evidence on whether one treatment method works better than another) and (b) the fact that conditions in most experimental therapy studies are not representative of traditional or typical child therapy in clinics makes it difficult to know whether the findings generalize to conventional clinic-based therapy.

NOTES

1. Although all such studies are *eligible* for inclusion, some important studies are inevitably omitted because they are not found. One major concern is that the technology available to meta-analysts makes it possible to do a rather comprehensive survey of published journal articles but not of outcome studies that are published only in book form.

2. In our article (Weisz, Weiss, Alicke, & Klotz, 1987) we mistakenly reported that 108 studies were included; three studies that were ultimately excluded from our analyses had been mistakenly retained in our bibliography.

4

EFFECTS OF CHILD PSYCHOTHERAPY: II. SPECIALLY FOCUSED META-ANALYSES AND REVIEWS

In Chapter 3 we surveyed the findings of broad-based meta-analyses covering a rather comprehensive array of child problems and approaches to therapy. Now we turn to more specialized meta-analyses and focused literature reviews intended to address rather specific questions about therapy effects.

THE HAZELRIGG, COOPER, AND BORDUIN (1987) META-ANALYSIS OF FAMILY THERAPY OUTCOME RESEARCH

The first focused meta-analysis we will review concerns children but only as a part of their family constellation. We refer here to a meta-analysis of family therapy effects carried out by Hazelrigg, Cooper, and Borduin (1987). Family therapy is an important part of the mental health care picture for children. When Kazdin, Siegel, and Bass (1990) asked 1,162 child mental health professionals about their work and their views on various treatment approaches, the respondents indicated that they spent an average of 12% of their time doing family therapy; 57% of all respondents rated family therapy as useful, and 59% rated it as effective.

Most previous reviews (Gurman, Kniskern, & Pinsof [1986] listed 22 reviews [some unpublished and some overlapping]; Hazelrigg et al. [1987] listed 10 separate published reviews) reached relatively positive conclusions about the efficacy of family therapy; however, there is disagreement on a few points. Although most reviews have concluded that family therapy is more effective than no therapy, at least two reviewers (Russell, Olson, Sprenkle, & Atilano [1983] and Wells & Dezen [1978]) refused to draw any conclusion about efficacy because of methodological concerns and inconsistency in findings across studies. Beyond the question of efficacy per se, reviewers have disagreed about whether family therapy is more effective than alternative approaches (see, for example, Ulrici [1983] vs. DeWitt [1978]). Hazelrigg et al. (1987) argued that differing conclusions across the various reviews resulted, in part, from difficulty that reviewers faced in synthesizing the family therapy data base by using traditional narrative review methods. Prompted by this concern, Hazelrigg et al. set out to capitalize on the synthesizing advantages of meta-analytic procedures.

Hazelrigg et al. (1987) defined *family therapy* as intervention involving at least one parent and one child and using procedures intended to produce change in the families' interactions. Relevant studies were sought through the reference lists of previous family therapy reviews and through computer data bases (*Psychological Abstracts* and *Educational Resources Information Center*) in which the term *family therapy* was crossed with *outcomes, results, effects, evaluation,* and *impact.* Hazelrigg et al. found 20 relevant studies (reported in 24 articles) that used methodology they considered to be acceptable (twice that number were excluded because of concerns about their methodology).

Subjects and treatment methods. Most of the studies included children and/or adolescents with behavior problems. Two studies included adolescent offenders. An additional three studies included adolescents and/or adults who were referred for and/or were receiving inpatient hospital treatment. Across the studies, sample sizes ranged from 11 to 4,303 (in Schubert & Miller, 1981). Many approaches to family therapy have been described in the literature, and a number of these were, no doubt, represented in the pool of studies reviewed; however, the particular approaches used were not described in the Hazelrigg report perhaps because the numbers would not have been sufficient to permit comparison of different approaches.

Effect size computation. ES computation involved procedures similar to those used by Casey and Berman (1985) as described in Chapter 3. The difference between the mean posttherapy scores of the family therapy group and the comparison group was divided by the average or common *SD* of the groups. When multiple effects were reported for a single study, these were averaged to produce a single overall ES. Mean ES across studies was calculated by averaging separate ES values from each study after these had been weighted by the study sample size. In addition, Hazelrigg et al. reported a *fail-safe N* (i.e., the number of studies that would sum to a null effect, which would need to be added to the existing pool of studies to reduce the overall effect size to nonsignificance). Rosenthal (1979) referred to this statistic as a measure of "tolerance for future null results" (p. 638).

Findings. Hazelrigg et al. first computed ES for the 10 studies in their pool that compared family therapy to no-treatment control groups. Seven of these studies included family interaction measures, and for these studies the mean ES for such measures was 0.45; this ES means that 67% of the people in the no-treatment conditions scored lower on family interaction measures than did the average family therapy client in the therapy groups. Although this ES was positive and statistically significant ($p < .03$) when the authors used a one-tailed test, the fail-safe *N* was only 3. In other words, only three studies involving null findings would be needed to reduce the ES to nonsignificance. Thus the finding could not be very reliable.

The results were stronger for comparisons involving behavior rating measures of outcome. The six studies using such measures showed a mean ES of 0.50; 69% of people in the no-treatment conditions scored lower on the behavior rating measures than did the average family therapy client in these studies. The ES was highly significant ($p < .0002$), and the fail-safe *N* was 26.

Only two studies were found that included follow-up data comparing family therapy to no-treatment conditions. The two studies yielded effect sizes of 1.45 and 0.37. Clearly, researchers in this area need to devote more attention to follow-up.

Less relevant to the main purpose of this book were Hazelrigg et al.'s analyses of the 11 studies that compared family therapy to other forms of therapy (individual, group, or medication). However, we will describe the results in brief. The three studies of this type that used family interaction measures generated a mean posttherapy ES of 0.31. The four studies that used behavior ratings showed a mean ES of 0.90. Follow-up data from studies that used recidivism (whether subjects returned to treatment) as the outcome measure showed a mean ES of 0.47, but follow-up studies that used other measures showed a negligible ES of 0.06.

To summarize, the findings pointed to positive effects of family therapy, but the small number of studies (and in some cases, modest sample sizes) involved in some of the comparisons makes some of the findings unreliable, as reflected in the fail-safe N statistic. The ES was fairly reliable for family therapy versus no-therapy when effects were measured by behavior ratings, but the ES was considerably less reliable when effects were measured by family interaction assessments. Follow-up data for therapy versus no-therapy comparisons were available from only two studies. The available data on family therapy versus alternative therapies generally pointed to superiority of family therapy, but no two studies used the same alternative therapy, and this makes the comparisons difficult to summarize simply. Surveying their findings, Hazelrigg et al. concluded, "In general, the results of this review are consistently favorable toward family therapy" (1987, p. 438).

THE DURLAK, FUHRMAN, AND LAMPMAN (1991) META-ANALYSIS OF COGNITIVE-BEHAVIORAL THERAPY OUTCOME RESEARCH

Next we consider a meta-analysis focused on an increasingly prominent form of child psychotherapy: cognitive-behavioral therapy. In the Kazdin, Siegel, and Bass (1990) survey of practicing child clinicians, cognitive approaches were deemed "useful" by 49% and "effective" by 50%. In a separate review of 223 child therapy outcome studies, Kazdin, Bass, et al. (1990) found that 22% of the studies involved cognitive-behavioral interventions. In the context of these findings, it is particularly useful to have the recent meta-analysis of cognitive-behavioral therapy effects by Durlak, Fuhrman, and Lampman (1991).

To identify relevant studies, Durlak et al. searched the literature from 1970 through March 1987. They used three search methods: (a) hand searching 15 relevant journals, (b) reviewing reference lists from identified studies and from reviews of cognitive-behavioral research, and (c) conducting a computer search of *Dissertation Abstracts International* (key terms used in the search not specified). Following Kendall (1981), Durlak et al. defined *cognitive-behavioral therapy* as "treatment that seeks overt behavioral change by teaching children to change thoughts and thought processes in an overt, active manner" (Durlak et al., 1991, p. 205). To be included in the meta-analysis, studies had to involve treatment that met this definition and a control group that represented the same population as treated youngsters. In addition, treatment had to be focused on modifying children's maladaptive behavioral or social functioning. Accordingly, the review excluded studies focused on academic outcomes and studies aimed at enhancing the performance of normal children. The review included only children whose mean age was 13 or younger and children who received individually administered therapy; thus studies in which therapy was administered in group form through parent or teacher consultation or within family therapy were not included in the review. A total of 64 studies (49 published articles, 15 unpublished dissertations) were ultimately included in the meta-analysis.

Subjects and their problems. The various studies included from 11 to 134 youngsters, with a mean sample size of 41. The age range was 4 to 13, with a mean age of 9.2, and 68% of the subjects were boys. Externalizing problems were the focus of treatment in 66% of the cases, internalizing problems in 17%, and mixed symptomatology in the remainder.

Treatment methods. Although all treatments were cognitive-behavioral, there was considerable variability in which cognitive-behavioral interventions were employed and in such other dimensions of treatment as modality and setting. Individual therapy sessions were employed in 53% of the studies, group sessions in 41%, and mixed modalities in 6%. Treatment most often occurred in regular school settings (68%), sometimes in residential centers (19%) and outpatient settings (6%). Number of treatment sessions ranged from 1 to 120, with a mean of 12.5, and the average duration in hours was 9.6. About three fourths of the studies used multiple forms of cognitive-behavioral therapy—for example, social skills training plus self-talk plus role playing. Indeed, a frequency distribution displayed by the authors indicated that 31 of the 64 studies used three or more specific types of cognitive-behavioral intervention in their treatment, and 17 of these studies used four or more.

Effect size computation. ES figures were calculated by using procedures similar to those of Casey and Berman (1985; reviewed in Chapter 3). The control group mean was subtracted from the treatment group mean, and the difference was divided by the pooled (treatment and control group) *SD*. As in Hedges and Olkin (1985), effect sizes were weighted according to study sample size. After finding that ES was not related to type of outcome measure, Durlak et al. decided to pool findings across measures within each study in order to generate a single mean ES per study. In addition to these ES values, Durlak et al. computed *normative effect size* (NES) figures for those studies involving clinical samples. NES provides an index of how a treatment or control group compares to some normative (nonclinical) group on measures of interest; thus NES can be used as an indicator of clinical significance—for example, the extent to which the posttreatment mean of a therapy group resembles that of a normal comparison group that was never considered to be in need of treatment. NES is calculated for any measure by subtracting the mean for the normative group from the mean for the treatment or control group and then dividing by the normative group *SD*.

Findings. Across the 64 studies, Durlak et al. found a mean ES of 0.56, indicating that after treatment the average treated child scored better than 71% of untreated youngsters, pooling across outcome measures. At follow-up the mean ES was 0.50, which placed the average treated child at the 69th percentile of the untreated group. Durlak et al. also found statistically significant heterogeneity of ES values across the 64 studies. This finding led to a test of their hypothesis that differences in ES would be associated with cognitive developmental level; specifically Durlak et al. argued that, in light of the emphasis in cognitive-behavioral therapy on the development and use of cognitive strategies to mediate behavior, youngsters who are more advanced in cognitive developmental level would profit more from this family of treatments. The evidence showed some support for this hypothesis. The mean ES for studies with children aged 11 to 13 (labeled the *formal operations* group by Durlak et al.) was 0.92, significantly higher than the mean of 0.55 for 7- to 11-year-olds (labeled the *concrete operations* group) and nonsignificantly higher than the mean of 0.57 for 5- to 7-year-olds (labeled the *preoperations* group). Homogeneity tests indicated that the three age groups differed but that ES was homogeneous within each group. Thus evidence supported the hypothesis that age (or developmental level) is a moderator of cognitive-behavioral therapy effects.

Another hypothesis advanced by Durlak et al. was that changes in behavior would be linked to changes in cognitive processes. The hypothesis is quite important because a major assumption underlying cognitive-behavioral therapy is that behavioral change is brought about through the medium of cognitive change. This notion was tested by examining the correlation between cognitive changes and behavioral changes in studies where both types of change were assessed. Across the 33 studies that met this criterion, there was a nonsignificant *negative* correlation ($r = -.22$) between cognitive changes and behavioral changes. This finding, of course, raises an intriguing question about just what the mechanism of change may actually be in cognitive-behavioral intervention and even whether the name given to this form of therapy is completely appropriate.

Finally Durlak et al. examined the clinical or practical significance of therapy effects for 23 studies involving clinical samples. NES figures (see above) were calculated to assess the extent to which treatment group means on normed measures moved toward means for nonclinical norm groups as a function of therapy. Results were especially encouraging for measures of personality (e.g., anxiety, depression, self-esteem) and cognitive tempo (e.g., reflection vs. impulsivity); on measures of both types, treatment groups scored more than 1 *SD* more severe than norm groups at the outset of treatment but were actually slightly better off than norm groups at the end of treatment. By contrast, on rating scales and checklists designed to reflect actual problem behavior, treated youngsters began treatment about 2 *SD* above normal group means and ended treatment 1.38 *SD* above those means. Because this change did not bring treated children's means within 1 *SD* of normal children, conventional standards would indicate that the change achieved in problem behavior was not clinically significant, averaged across studies. On the other hand, when all three types of outcome measures were combined, treatment group scores shifted from 1.55 *SD* at treatment outset to 0.50 *SD* at treatment termination, and this is considered to be clinically significant change.

THE RUSSELL, GREENWALD, AND SHIRK (1991) META-ANALYSIS OF LANGUAGE CHANGE IN CHILD PSYCHOTHERAPY

The third focused meta-analysis we will consider addressed a dimension that is often interwoven with child psychopathology: language proficiency. As the authors (Russell, Greenwald, & Shirk, 1991) pointed out, half the youngsters who have language disorders also have some psychological disorder (see Baker & Cantwell, 1987), and more than a fourth of clinic-referred children turn out to have some language disorder as well (see Cohen, Davine, & Meloche-Kelly, 1989). Moreover, significant language problems that are closely linked to the *DSM-III-R* pervasive developmental disorders (e.g., autistic disorder) and specific developmental disorders (e.g., developmental receptive and expressive language disorders) constitute a substantial proportion of treated young people (Tuma & Pratt, 1982). Finally, some research (e.g., Richman & Lindgren, 1981) suggests that language plays a mediating role in the development of behavioral self-regulation and self-control. For these reasons, Russell et al. (1991) set out to assess the extent to which child therapy affected child language proficiency. For this purpose, Russell et al. searched the pool of studies included in the Weisz, Weiss, Alicke, and Klotz (1987) meta-analysis (see Chapter 3), identifying 18 studies that included at least one language-linked outcome measure. Across the 18 studies, there were 26 treatment-control comparisons (several studies had multiple treatment groups).

Subjects and their problems. Subjects in the studies selected were similar to the Weisz et al. full sample in age ($M = 9.8$, $SD = 3.7$), percentage of boys (78.9), and percentage treated for overcontrolled, undercontrolled, or "other" problems. Specific problems treated included a rather broad range (e.g., hyperactivity, anxiety, misconduct). In light of the selection criteria originally employed by Weisz, Weiss, Alicke, and Klotz (1987), the sample did not include youngsters referred only for "underdeveloped reading, writing, or knowledge of specific school subjects" (Weisz, Weiss, Alicke, & Klotz, 1987, p. 544). The sample also did not include any children described as suffering from psychotic or pervasive developmental disorders or from mental retardation.

Treatment methods. The mean number of treatment sessions across the 26 comparisons was 18.7 ($SD = 10.6$). Focusing on descriptions of therapy reported in the studies, Russell et al. selected three types of verbal processes for special attention: (a) "spontaneous verbal interaction in process-oriented therapy" (1991, p. 917; e.g., nondirective, insight oriented); (b) "verbal interaction constrained by preset tasks and problem-solving and self-instructional training" (p. 917; e.g., self- instructional training); and (c) "behavioral exchanges in which verbal interaction plays a secondary role, as in operant and counterconditioning" (p. 917). Each treatment condition in the studies sampled was classified (with 100% reliability) according to which of the three types was involved.

Effect size computation. ES values were computed by using the same procedure used by Weisz, Weiss, Alicke, and Klotz (1987). The control group mean was subtracted from the treatment group mean, and the difference was divided by the *SD* of the control group. Effect sizes were computed separately for each treatment group.

Findings. Across the 26 treatment-control comparisons, the overall ES for language proficiency measures was 0.32, significantly different from 0 only at the 0.05 level. The average treated child scored at the 63rd percentile of the untreated group. Effects were not reliably different for expressive/receptive language measures versus reading proficiency measures; however, both language proficiencies were significantly more affected by therapy than were nonlanguage measures in the same studies (but language and nonlanguage change were correlated 0.39). Interestingly, the amount of language change was significantly correlated with number of therapy sessions ($r = .45$), but the amount of change on nonlanguage measures was not ($r = .15$).

Treatment modality made a big difference in the magnitude of effects. Children who received individual therapy showed a mean language change ES of 1.31, more than 10 times the effect of other therapy modalities combined. The authors speculated that this change may have occurred because individual sessions require more concentrated language interaction between child and therapist than do other modalities. In addition, they suggested that the large ES may reflect modeling opportunities and reduction of anxiety associated with verbal activity, both of which may occur to a greater extent in individual sessions.

As noted earlier, the authors coded treatments into three types of verbal process. When they examined ES as a function of these three types, they found marked differences. Treatments classified as involving spontaneous verbal interaction generated a mean ES of 1.24, about 4 times as large as the ES for treatments involving behavioral exchange (mean ES = 0.35) and more than 10 times as large as the ES for treatments involving verbal interactions constrained by goal-oriented formats (mean ES = 0.08). Note, however, that none of these differences was statistically significant. Overall, although low power may have interfered with detection of some potentially important group differences, the findings do suggest that the psychotherapy procedures assessed in this pool of 26 studies had measurable positive effects on language proficiency.

THE WEISS AND WEISZ (1990) META-ANALYSIS
OF EFFECTS OF METHODOLOGICAL FACTORS

Critics of meta-analyses (e.g., Kazdin, 1983; Wilson, 1985) have expressed concern that such analyses often include studies with methodological limitations and that this may limit the validity of the summary results. We addressed this and related concerns via a meta-analysis (Weiss & Weisz, 1990) focused on the impact of various methodological factors on meta-analytic findings. In essence, we conducted a series of analyses, using the pool of studies from our 1987 meta-analysis (Weisz, Weiss, Alicke, & Klotz, 1987) and assessing the extent to which the findings might have been influenced by methodological variables.

The search procedures and exclusionary criteria for Weisz, Weiss, Alicke, and Klotz (1987) were described in Chapter 3. There we also described the sample of 105 studies, the subject populations employed, the target problems treated, and the range of treatment methods employed. In addition, we detailed the methods used to calculate ES estimates. All this information applies to the Weiss and Weisz (1990) methodological meta-analysis.

Overview of data analytic procedures. To deal with the inherent problem of confounding of variables, we used interaction and eliminating tests similar to those used in Weisz, Weiss, Alicke, and Klotz (1987; see description in Chapter 3). We first tested each of the validity variables (e.g., whether subjects were randomly assigned to groups; see others below) as main effects, with outcome as dependent variable. When any main effect thus tested was significant, we statistically eliminated (i.e., controlled for; see Appelbaum & Cramer, 1974) the other validity factors one at a time to test whether the main effect might have resulted from confounding with other validity factors. Next we tested interactions to assess whether the validity factors influenced relations between other variables and outcome. We tested interactions between each validity factor and each of the three factors that had been found to be significantly related to outcome in our previous meta-analysis (Weisz, Weiss, Alicke, & Klotz, 1987): age, treatment type (behavioral vs. nonbehavioral), and source of outcome measure (e.g., parents, teachers, subject performance). Our analyses addressed the impact of methodological variables in three categories: (a) type of control group, (b) internal validity dimensions, and (c) external validity dimensions.

Findings: I. Type of control group. The literature contains considerable discussion about the most appropriate type of control group for child therapy outcome research. All the child therapy meta-analyses have included studies that differ from one another in type of control group, yet we have had little information on whether this variation makes a difference. We coded control groups into four categories: (a) *assessment only* (subjects had no contact with investigators except for pre- and postassessments), (b) *waiting list* (subjects placed on a list and told that they could receive therapy at the end of the control period), (c) *attention-placebo* (contact time roughly equated to that of the therapy group but consisting largely of undirected interaction with therapist or other children), and (d) *minimal treatment* (general, nonspecific treatment relative to the goals of the study). Our analyses did not reveal any significant difference in ES across studies as a function of the type of control group used. Nor did the four types of control group differ in the degree to which their scores on outcome measures changed from pre- to postassessment. However, control groups did show significant improvement in scores from pre to post, indicating that it is not only treated children who show gains over the course of the average outcome study.

Findings: II. Impact of internal validity variables. Several variables were identified as possible threats to the internal validity of outcome studies. Under *experimental attrition,* we recorded the percentage of control group and treatment group subjects who failed to complete posttreatment assessment. We found that attrition was marginally higher for treatment groups (5.5%) than for control groups (4.2%), that the correlation between treatment and control group attrition was quite high (r = .76), and that neither treatment group attrition nor control group attrition was significantly related to the outcome of studies. Moreover, neither attrition measure showed a significant interaction with any of the substantive variables (age, treatment type, source of outcome measure).

Under *subject assignment,* we noted whether individual subjects were assigned to treatment and control groups nonrandomly, randomly without any matching of treatment and control groups on such characteristics as age or gender, or randomly with matching on at least one subject characteristic. We found a significant main effect of subject assignment on outcome, with the highest mean ES for random with matching (1.04), next highest for random without matching (0.80), and the lowest for nonrandom assignment (0.34). When we tested the robustness of this effect in a series of analyses eliminating each of the other validity factors, no eliminating test reduced the subject assignment effect to nonsignificance. Moreover, not one of the interaction tests was significant. Thus the effect of the subject assignment variable was quite robust. We also found that matching made a substantial difference in the similarity of groups at pretreatment; when treatment and control groups were not matched, they differed by 0.12 SD ($p < .05$) at pretreatment, but when matched, they differed by only 0.02 (ns) at pretreatment.

We also coded studies along three dimensions relevant to reactivity, or the potential of their outcome measures to produce biasing effects on subjects. We used a 4-point scale to rate studies on *reactivity I: measurement technology*—that is, following Shapiro and Shapiro (1982), the degree to which their outcome measures were "soft" (high likelihood of subjective bias; e.g., self-ratings of symptoms) versus "hard" (low likelihood of bias). We found that "harder" outcome measures were associated with higher mean ES. Most of the eliminating tests and all of the interaction tests left this effect unscathed (or at least still significant). However, controlling for the *professional clinician* variable (see below) and later for *rater blindness* (see below) reduced the main effect of this reactivity I measure to nonsignificance; this reduction suggests that the main effect was due partly to its overlap with these other factors.

We also coded studies for *reactivity II: rater blindness*—that is, whether outcome data came from a person who was either aware or not aware of whether the subject had been in a treated or untreated group. This variable had no reliable effect on outcomes, nor did it interact significantly with any of the substantive variables.

Our other internal validity factor was *reactivity III: subject blindness*. Here we coded not whether subjects were aware of their own group assignment, but rather whether they were aware that an outcome assessment was being carried out. Such an awareness, we reasoned, might cause the child to behave in an unrepresentative way. We did indeed find that studies using experimentally blind youngsters produced significantly smaller effect sizes than nonblind studies. Of all the eliminating and ignoring tests, only one had a substantial impact: When *subject assignment* (random, etc.) was controlled, the subject blindness effect became nonsignificant.

Findings: III. Impact of external validity variables. Following Kazdin (1978), we included another cluster of variables that seemed potentially relevant to the external (or "ecological") validity of findings. One variable, *treated anyway,* referred to the question of whether subjects in a study would have been in some form of psychological or behavioral treatment regardless of the research project (vs. having been simply recruited for treatment from, say, a group of normal school children). Under a second variable, *professional therapist,* we coded whether those who conducted the treatment did clinical work as their primary vocation (vs. being primarily graduate students, university faculty members, etc.). Under the third variable, *setting,* we coded whether treatment took place in a clinical setting (e.g., hospital or community clinic) or nonclinical setting (e.g., school). Our main effect and interaction tests yielded no significant effects involving any of these three external validity variables.

Findings IV: Overall effect of the validity variables. We assessed the overall impact of the validity factors by computing a multiple regression equation with ES as the criterion and all eight of the validity variables (internal and external) as the predictors. The analysis indicated that the combination of validity factors accounted for a small but statistically significant 7% of the variance in ES. For comparison purposes, we computed another multiple regression equation with ES as the criterion, this time including as predictors the seven substantive variables that had shown significant main effects in our earlier meta-analysis (Weisz, Weiss, Alicke, & Klotz, 1987). These variables together accounted for 11% of the variance in ES. Thus the validity variables, taken together, accounted for about two thirds as much of the ES variance as was accounted for by substantive factors in the original meta-analysis.

Findings V: A "fantasy analysis." Finally, we carried out a "fantasy analysis," estimating the magnitude of the effect one might obtain if one could conduct a "methodologically ideal" experiment. In such an experiment, one might use clinic-referred children, treated by professional clinicians, in a clinic, using random assignment and matching, without any attrition, using blind raters and subjects, and assessing outcome via the least reactive measures (e.g., GPA, arrests). We produced an estimate of the ES from such a study by using the model parameter estimates derived from the regression equation and then computing the predicted value for a study having the "most valid" level of each validity factor. The predicted ES generated by this method was 1.14, considerably higher than the actual ES found in Weisz, Weiss,

PERCENTILE

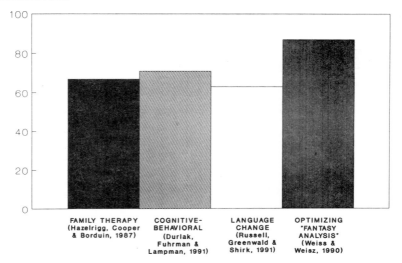

Figure 4.1. Main Effects Reported in Four Specially Focused Meta-Analyses

Alicke, and Klotz (1987) or indeed the ES values found in any other child meta-analysis (see Chapter 3). This "optimizing ES" would place the average treated child at the 87th percentile of the untreated comparison group. Figure 4.1 shows the result of this analysis, compared to the findings of the focused meta-analyses reviewed earlier in this chapter. What the optimizing analysis suggests indirectly is that methodological inadequacies in studies reviewed in the meta-analyses thus far have not artificially inflated the effects of child psychotherapy; instead these limitations have very likely *reduced* estimates of the impact of therapy. Eliminating the limitations, our analysis suggests, would very likely increase estimates of therapy impact.

THE GREENWALD AND RUSSELL (1991) EVALUATION OF RATIONALES FOR INCLUSIVENESS IN META-ANALYTIC SAMPLES

The Weiss and Weisz (1990) findings suggest that methodological variations may have at least a modest impact on the effect sizes generated in meta-analyses. This information leads quite logically to the question of whether meta-analysts should seek to include all studies relevant to the area they are reviewing or should include only studies that meet certain criteria for methodological rigor. In general, meta-analysts have followed the former strategy (see one rationale in Smith et al., 1980, who favored inclusiveness), but Greenwald and Russell (1991), among others, have argued for the latter approach. To support their argument, Greenwald and Russell (1991) carried out an empirical evaluation of six rationales for inclusiveness.

For this evaluation Greenwald and Russell used a subset of the studies surveyed in the Weisz, Weiss, Alicke, and Klotz (1987) meta-analysis. From the original pool of 105 studies, they selected 24 (including 29 treatment-control comparisons). No information was provided about why only 24 studies were selected or the criteria used to select these particular studies.

The 24 studies were coded "for the presence vs. absence of eight methodological problems that commonly threaten the construct, internal, and external validity of psychotherapy outcome studies" (Greenwald & Russell, 1991, p. 2): (a) *lack of random assignment* (to treatment and control groups), (b) *evaluation bias* (experimenters know subjects' group assignment when outcomes are assessed), (c) *unequal concurrent treatments* (subjects receive some treatment in addition to the experimental treatment, with no control for the additional treatment), (d) *unequal attrition* (the number of subjects who drop out of a treatment group is 10% greater than the number who drop out of the control group), (e) *inexperienced therapist* (the therapist is in training, e.g., in graduate school), (f) *mono-operationalism* (only one outcome variable is measured), (g) *insufficient amount of treatment* (treatment involved < 10 sessions), and (h) *lack of treatment integrity* (scored as present "if there was no mention of a treatment manual or the treatment was not taped and periodically reviewed" [Greenwald & Russell, 1991, p. 3]).

Ratings on these eight problem dimensions were used to address the six rationales the authors identified as bases for inclusiveness. We will summarize the data that were brought to bear on each of the rationales:

Rationale 1: *Different investigators cannot agree on the relative importance of inclusion/exclusion criteria.* To address this rationale, the authors had five methodologically oriented psychologists independently rate the seriousness of each of the eight threats to validity listed above, using a 1-6 Likert scale (6 = most severe). On these severity ratings, according to Greenwald and Russell, "the reliability of the typical judge was 0.56; the effective reliability of the full set of judges was 0.86, providing evidence that the severity ratings of these judges can be considered to be reliable" (p. 3). Greenwald and Russell did not indicate how these reliability figures (including those for "the typical judge") were calculated or precisely what statistic these figures represent; however, the authors did conclude from the data that Rationale 1, above, is invalid. Readers may be interested to know that the mean severity ratings were 6.0 for *lack of random assignment,* 5.6 for *unequal concurrent treatments,* 5.0 for *evaluation bias,* 4.2 for *unequal attrition,* 3.8 for *insufficient treatment,* 3.8 for *lack of treatment integrity,* 2.8 for *mono-operationalism,* and 2.4 for *inexperienced therapist.*

Rationale 2: *Methodological quality cannot be reliably assessed.* Some evidence in support of this rationale was provided by McGuire et al. (1985). However, Greenwald and Russell offered counterevidence. When they had two coders rate each of the 24 studies for the presence or absence of each of the eight threats to validity, the coders achieved statistically significant kappas ($p < .05$) on six of the eight dimensions. The two nonsignificant kappas were found for *unequal attrition* (0.33) and *evaluation bias* (0.34). Kappas for *unequal concurrent treatments* and *inexperienced therapists* were significant but low (0.45 and 0.48, respectively). Kappas for the other four dimensions ranged from 0.61 to 0.89. An overall index of global methodological quality was computed for each study, and two raters' judgments on this index correlated 0.68. Greenwald and Russell concluded that reliable judgments "can be obtained by assessing individual threats to validity, and by devising a sensitive global methodological weight based on these individual threats" (p. 4).

Rationale 3: *Effect size and methodological quality do not covary* (see Smith et al., 1980; Shapiro & Shapiro, 1983). To evaluate this rationale, Greenwald and Russell computed the correlation between their global methodological quality ratings for each study (see preceding paragraph) and the study effect sizes. The resulting coefficient was only 0.23; however, the authors "disattenuated" this coefficient for the levels of reliability of the raters and for the estimated reliability of the outcome measures and reported a coefficient of 0.39. These results, like those of the last Weiss and Weisz (1990) analysis, reported above, suggest that effect size may be significantly and positively related to methodological quality. This possible relationship, in turn, suggests that very inclusive meta-analyses generate relatively conservative estimates of the effects produced by psychotherapy.

Rationale 4: *Design flaws in a study are randomly distributed.* The idea underlying this rationale is that "not all studies would suffer from the same flaw or combination of flaws, so that ultimately 'many weak studies can add up to a strong conclusion' (Smith et al., 1980, p. 49)" (Greenwald & Russell, 1991, p. 2). To address this rationale, Greenwald and Russell computed polychoric correlations among all possible pairs of their eight threats to validity. Of the 28 coefficients, 9 were significant, indicating at least some covariation among some of the validity threats. Some of the significant correlations carried interesting implications. For example, a very strong negative relationship between *insufficient treatment* and *mono-operationalism* (−0.95) suggested that as less treatment was provided, more variables were used to measure outcome, and vice versa.

Rationale 5: *By including all the relevant studies and describing their characteristics, the meta-analyst makes it possible to assess the impact of such moderator variables as design quality* (Smith et al., 1980). To address this rationale, Greenwald and Russell offered calculations indicating that for meta-analyses with small samples (e.g., their sample of 24 studies) and several methodological flaws to be considered separately, assessment of the impact of design moderator variables would likely have reliability problems and low power. The alternative of examining the relation between effect size and a global summary index of methodological quality might not be workable, the authors argued, because of such problems as scores being non-normally distributed across the array of studies.

Rationale 6: *Even a very inclusive sample will certainly exclude many relevant studies—especially those that did not yield significant findings and were not accepted for publication—so any further shrinkage of the sample (e.g., by excluding studies with imperfect methodology) would exacerbate the "file drawer" problem* (see Rosenthal, 1979). The problem of concern is that meta-analyses may not provide a representative look at what has been found because many studies (e.g., unpublished ones, those rejected because of methodological limitations) remain in file drawers rather than entering the sample. The risk, as Rosenthal (1979) put it, is "that the journals are filled with the 5% of studies that show Type I errors, while the file drawers back at the lab are filled with the 95% of the studies that show nonsignificant (e.g., $p < 0.05$) results"

(p. 638). Greenwald and Russell addressed this issue by computing a fail-safe N; they estimated that it would take 390 studies averaging null results to reduce the p level of the average effect size for their sample of 24 studies to nonsignificance. From this finding, they concluded that it is inappropriate to raise "the specter of the file drawer problem" to justify inclusiveness in sampling.

To summarize, Greenwald and Russell offered empirically based arguments in an effort to refute each of six possible rationales for inclusive sampling in meta-analyses. In their view, none of these rationales is well supported. They maintain that sampling needs to be guided by stricter methodological criteria. What remains unclear, however, is *how* strict one should be if one wishes to follow the Greenwald-Russell perspective in selecting a sample. One could certainly require such pristine designs that virtually no study could survive the purge. Anything short of a truly pristine standard requires the application of a particular meta-analyst's value system, an inevitably subjective process. For this reason we continue to lean toward relatively inclusive samples (as in Weisz, Weiss, Alicke, & Klotz, 1987) that are carefully analyzed for the impact of methodological variations (as in Weiss & Weisz, 1990). Finally, we remind the reader that both our analyses (in Weiss & Weisz, 1990) and the Greenwald-Russell (1991) analysis indicate that the overall effect of using very inclusive samples, accepting studies with certain methodological limitations, is to generate conservative estimates—that is, *underestimates*—of the "true effect" of therapy. Evidently, including studies that have some methodological limitations does *not* lead to unrealistic overstatements of therapy effects.

BARRNETT, DOCHERTY, AND FROMMELT'S (1991) REVIEW OF OUTCOME RESEARCH WITH NONBEHAVIORAL THERAPIES

Barrnett, Docherty, and Frommelt (1991) reviewed child outcome studies that employed nonbehavioral treatment methods. The search procedures were not described in the report, but the authors did note that, to be included in the review, studies had to (a) have at least one group that was treated via individual therapy, (b) "include at least one comparison group" (control group or alternate treatment), and (d) involve some intervention that was not behavioral, cognitive-behavioral, family, group, or pharmacological. The review covered 43 studies published between 1963 and 1988; however, all but four of the studies were published before 1974, and only one was published in the 1980s. The sample included 13 studies with grade schoolers, 10 with junior high and/or high school students, 10 with youngsters from both levels, and 10 with groups of unspecified grade level or age.

Only 21 of the articles (describing 17 different studies) involved comparison of treated versus untreated youngsters. Of the 21 articles, 12 reported more favorable outcomes for children receiving psychotherapy than for untreated children; 9 reported no significant group difference. In general, Barrnett et al. were critical of what they viewed as the less than rigorous methodology of many of the studies. In fact, they concluded that "summary impressions (e.g., about the efficacy of child therapy) cannot be made due to the magnitude of the flaws in basic psychotherapy research" (p. 1). This conclusion should be tempered somewhat by the fact that most of the studies Barrnett et al. reviewed were published more than two decades ago, prior to some significant advances in the sophistication of outcome research.

SUMMARY

In this chapter we complemented the broad, general meta-analyses of Chapter 3 with more specialized meta-analyses and reviews addressing more narrowly focused topics. Like the broad, general meta-analyses of the previous chapter, the three topically focused meta-analyses reviewed here pointed to significant positive overall effects of psychotherapy—when in the family therapy modality (Hazelrigg et al., 1987), when limited to the cognitive-behavioral approach (Durlak et al., 1991), and when examined exclusively for its effects on language (Russell et al., 1991). The Weiss and Weisz (1990) meta-analysis showed that certain methodological characteristics of therapy outcome studies are related, at least modestly, to the effect sizes those studies generate; collectively those characteristics accounted for 7% of the effect size variance in the Weisz, Weiss, Alicke, and Klotz (1987) broad-based meta-analysis. Greenwald and Russell's (1991) analysis suggested that some of the reasons meta-analysts have given for keeping their meta-analytic samples large and inclusive may not be as compelling as some have thought. And finally the Barrnett et al. (1991) survey and critique reminds us how much our field needs rigorous studies of the outcome of nonbehavioral forms of psychotherapy.

5

EFFECTS OF CHILD PSYCHOTHERAPY: III. STUDIES OF CLINIC-BASED AND COMMUNITY-BASED INTERVENTIONS

The meta-analyses reviewed in previous chapters show consistently positive overall effects of psychotherapy. Moreover, these meta-analyses reflect data from a large number of distinct outcome studies ($N > 250$) and subjects ($N > 13,000$). Thus it may be tempting to conclude that "the evidence" on child therapy effects is now in and that the news is very good: Psychotherapy works with children and adolescents. Unfortunately such a conclusion may be premature. To explain why, we need to examine the evidence that forms the basis of the meta-analyses.

As we noted at the end of Chapter 3, most of the outcome studies included in the meta-analyses appear to have involved children, interventions, and/or treatment conditions that may not be very representative of conventional clinical practice. In a large percentage of these controlled experimental studies, (a) youngsters were recruited for treatment, not actually clinic referred; (b) samples were selected for homogeneity on one or two focal problems, and treatment focused on the focal problem(s), quite different from the broad array of problems seen and treated in clinics; (c) therapists used only one or two therapeutic techniques and had recent training in the technique(s), quite different from the situation often faced by clinic therapists; and (d) therapy was guided by manuals and/or was closely monitored for treatment integrity, luxuries that are difficult to find in service-oriented clinics. Thus conditions in most child clinics may be different from (and less optimum than) the somewhat artificial conditions typically arranged for controlled outcome studies (see Persons, 1991, for a similar argument regarding psychotherapy in general).

Other differences between conventional clinic practice with children and child therapy outcome research have been noted by Kazdin, Siegel, and Bass (1990). When they surveyed 223 child outcome studies, Kazdin et al. found that child therapy research, unlike child clinical practice, tends to (a) focus on children recruited from and treated in schools, (b) employ group interventions rather than individual treatment, (c) use behavioral and cognitive-behavioral methods (rather than the psychodynamic, eclectic, and family-oriented approaches more often favored in clinics), (d) emphasize brief interventions averaging 8-10 weeks (vs. 27-55 weeks in clinical practice), (e) deemphasize involvement of parents and other family members, and (f) deemphasize consultation with teachers.

In several respects, then, it appears that the procedures and conditions associated with clinic-based therapy for children are rather different from those typically arranged for outcome research. Thus it is hard to gauge the extent to which the findings of meta-analyses based on that outcome research can be generalized to the clinic-based therapy and other community-based interventions that are provided to disturbed children in most communities. This difficulty suggests that an important question remains to be answered, a question to which we turn our attention in this chapter: Are the benefits of therapy as demonstrated in controlled outcome studies matched by effects of child therapy in clinic and community settings?

OUTCOME ASSESSMENT WITH CLINIC- AND COMMUNITY-BASED INTERVENTIONS

Although this may appear to be a rather straightforward question, a significant obstacle stands in the way of answering it: Legal and ethical constraints prevent clinics from randomly assigning people who apply for treatment to a no-treatment control condition. Other community-based intervention programs for children face similar constraints. Thus the rigorous comparisons of randomly selected treatment and no-treatment control groups, which are the forte of controlled, experimental outcome studies, are not likely to be possible very often in clinic and community settings[1] (for an interesting exception, however, see De Fries, Jenkins, & Williams [1964], discussed below).

To address this problem, several researchers have attempted to assess the outcomes of interventions by relying on alternative procedures that do not require random assignment of disturbed individuals to control groups. An influential early step in this direction was taken by Eysenck (1952) in a study of adult therapy effects. He assembled reported rates of improvement across 19 studies of "neurotic" adults treated with psychotherapy; these data were compared to estimated base rates of improvement in studies of neurotic adults treated more custodially in state hospitals. Treated adults' rate of improvement fell below the hospital base rate of 72% improvement, leading Eysenck to conclude that "the figures fail to support the hypothesis that psychotherapy facilitates recovery from neurotic disorder" (1952, p. 323). (But see also critiques of Eysenck's study, e.g., by Rosenzweig, 1954.)

Levitt (1957b) followed Eysenck's (1952) general procedure to estimate the effects of therapy for "neurotic" *children*. The base rate of improvement without treatment was estimated from two follow-up studies that included children who had dropped out after being accepted for clinic treatment (Lehrman, Sirluck, Black, & Glick, 1949; Witmer & Keller, 1942). To this base rate, Levitt compared the improvement rate reported for treated children in 18 published reports of outcome at treatment termination and 17 published reports of outcome at follow-up. The improvement rate was 72.5% for untreated children, 74% for treated children. These results, Levitt concluded, "fail to support the view that psychotherapy with 'neurotic' children is effective" (1957b, p. 195).

Like Eysenck's (1952) article, Levitt's (1957b) report stimulated a number of critiques (e.g., Barrett, Hampe, & Miller, 1978; Eisenberg & Gruenberg, 1961; Halpern, 1968; Heinicke & Goldman, 1960; Hood-Williams, 1960). Among the criticisms were these: (a) Significant numbers of children who formed the no-treatment base rate sample may not have been seriously disturbed (some had been referred initially only for diagnostic services); (b) it may not be accurate to assume that the no-treatment group received no intervention because for some children "the diagnostic process itself constitutes an intense, short-term therapeutic process" (Barrett et al., 1978, p. 412); (c) comparing improvement rates in treated and untreated children from studies conducted in very different years may be problematic because of time-linked shifts in caseloads, types of children seen in clinics, therapeutic methods, and so on; and (d) for comparisons to be meaningful, treated and untreated children may need to be matched on such variables as maturational gradients, neuropsychological functioning, and psychosocial factors (Halpern, 1968).

A number of the criticisms of Levitt (1957b) were related to the fact that the base rates of improvement for treated and "untreated" individuals were estimated from different studies and thus different clinic settings, with different admission criteria and different population bases. Because the comparisons were made across studies (rather than within studies), it was not possible to assess directly the demographic, developmental, or clinical similarity of the treated and untreated groups being compared. The treatment-no treatment comparisons thus were rather indirect, as Levitt recognized, and the possibility of initial uncontrolled group differences remained unexamined. Other studies, though, have involved more direct and precise comparisons between treated and untreated children in clinic and community settings. We turn now to those studies.

COMPARISON OF TREATED CHILDREN
TO MATCHED CHILDREN FROM A POPULATION SURVEY:
THE BUCKINGHAMSHIRE CHILD SURVEY
(SHEPHERD, OPPENHEIM, & MITCHELL, 1966)

One approach, taken by Shepherd, Oppenheim, and Mitchell (1966) as a part of the Buckinghamshire Child Survey, was to compare children treated in clinics to demographically and clinically matched unreferred, untreated children identified through a separate general population survey. The age range was 5-15 years (gender distribution not reported, although both genders were represented). The general population children were drawn from a 1-in-10 sample (every 10th child in county records) of children attending local authority schools in the county of Buckinghamshire, England.

The 50 clinic children (all treated for the first time) and the 50 nonclinic children were initially selected through pairwise matching on age, gender, and behavioral/problem profile; then the groups were compared and shown not to be significantly different on such demographic factors as parents' age, employment of mother, presence of young children in the household, or on clinicians' blind ratings of overall severity of the child's disturbance. Although no significant clinical differences were found between children in the two groups, a few differences were found among the parent variables. For example, mothers of clinic children, not surprisingly, reported higher levels of worry, puzzlement, and helplessness about their children's problems than mothers of nonclinic children; the latter were more likely to view their children's problems as temporary and not in need of professional intervention.

Shepherd et al. (1966) compared adjustment in the two groups 2 years after the initial assessments (and thus 2 years after clinic contact for the clinic group). To generate the follow-up data, in-home clinical interviews were conducted with 87 of the original 100, and improvement ratings were made by trained judges who were blind to the clinic-nonclinic status of the children. Shepherd et al. (1966) summarized their findings succinctly: "While 63% of the clinic cases had improved after 2 years, so had 61% of matched children who had not attended the clinics, and whose parents had at interview confirmed the existence of disturbed behavior" (p. 47). The researchers probed further to assess whether *extent* of treatment might differentiate those clinic children who had improved from those who had "deteriorated" in their level of adjustment over the 2 years. They found "virtually no difference in the average number of clinic attendances between those who improved and those who deteriorated" (p. 46). These two findings by Shepherd et al. (1966) do not provide any evidence that clinic treatment was effective.

A limitation of the Buckinghamshire study is that the children in its untreated sample were not actually referred for treatment. Mothers of these children, compared to the clinic mothers, showed significantly less distress over their children's problems and significantly more optimism that the problems were temporary. And, of course, there may have been other, undocumented differences between children and families who sought clinic treatment and those who did not. For this reason it is important to complement evidence such as the Buckinghamshire study with evidence on treated and untreated groups, *both* of whom initially sought clinic treatment.

CLINIC-BASED STUDIES COMPARING
THERAPY DROPOUTS TO THERAPY COMPLETERS

This brings us to another means of fashioning relatively direct and precise treatment versus no-treatment comparisons: comparing treated and untreated children admitted to the same treatment facilities in the same time period to untreated cases consisting of those who drop out prior to treatment. This approach addresses the problems associated with the use of nonreferred children (as in the Buckinghamshire study) and with the use of separate dropout and therapy completer groups (as in Levitt's [1957b] study). However, there still remains the important issue of whether dropouts and treatment completers differ from one another in important demographic or clinical variables. Hood-Williams (1960) suggested, for example, that treated groups may "represent the more serious, intractable problems, while at least a proportion of the untreated groups are minor or transient problems" (p. 84). If this were the case, then a comparison between dropouts and completers would not represent a fair test of the effect of treatment.

In reply to such criticisms, Levitt (1971) noted that the available evidence suggested that dropout and completer groups did not differ in the seriousness or chronicity of their problems. And as we note in Chapter 2 of this book, considerable research before and after Levitt's work has failed to generate much evidence of reliable, consistent differences between child therapy completers and dropouts (see also data from Gould et al., 1985; Levitt, 1957a; McAdoo & Roeske, 1973; Weisz, Weiss, & Langmeyer, 1987, 1989). The few differences that have been replicated at all tend to suggest that pretherapy prognosis may actually be slightly worse for children who drop out than for children who remain in treatment; such a trend, of course, would tend to bias outcome comparisons slightly in favor of treated samples over untreated dropouts.

In addition to relying on previous findings on the comparability of dropouts and therapy completers, investigators who wish to compare outcomes among treated children and those who drop out of treatment may test for pretherapy differences on clinical characteristics if relevant data are available. In light of such comparison procedures and the weight of previous evidence (see Chapter 2), children who drop out of treatment may be an acceptable (though certainly not ideal) naturally occurring control group for outcome research in circumstances where no randomly assigned control group can be constituted. In the next section, we examine four studies that use such an approach to outcome assessment.[2]

The Lehrman, Sirluck, Black, and Glick (1949) study of child guidance clinic treatment. Perhaps the most appropriate study of this type to begin with is one of the two that provided a "base rate" sample for the controversial Levitt (1957b) article (for information on the other base rate study, see Note 2, regarding Witmer & Keller, 1942). Lehrman et al. (1949) focused on a group of more than 300 youngsters seen at Jewish Board of Guardians (JBG) Child Guidance Clinics in New York prior to April, 1942. The youngsters were about two-thirds male and averaged 12.5 years of age (range: 3-20). Most of the referrals came from social agencies (25%), relatives other than parents (25%), and schools (24%), with an additional 10% from the courts, 8% from parents, and 8% from medical sources. About 60% of the cases were referred for "primary behavior disorder" (e.g., uncontrollable, hostile, destructive, or impulsive behavior), but an additional 25% were referred for "psychoneurosis," and other problems and disorders were represented as well.

Some 196 of the cases formed the treatment group; these were regarded as having been "totally treated" within the framework of the JBG system. The treatment was provided by psychiatric social workers who followed treatment plans developed by their clinical teams, each of which included a psychiatrist. Most of the treatment consisted of individual sessions, with all children receiving at least 5 sessions and 75% of them receiving more than 30 sessions. The foreword to the study, written by the chief consultant psychiatrist, suggested that the treatment procedures, labeled *transference psychotherapy*, were derived largely from psychoanalytic theory.

An additional 110 cases formed the control group. These cases had been observed by JBG staff and found to fit the criteria of eligibility for services but had not received a course of treatment at JBG clinics or elsewhere (usually because the youngster had been withdrawn by his or her parents). All those in the control group had been observed and had met with clinic staff, with some receiving as many as five sessions, but 25% received only one or two sessions.

Lehrman et al. compared the treatment and control groups on a small number of demographic, family, and clinical characteristics early in their contact with JBG clinics. The groups were found not to differ significantly in age or gender. A significant difference did indicate that a higher proportion of the control group than the treatment group had "two adequate parents." Finally, a significant ($p < .01$) group difference was found in the distribution of psychiatric diagnoses: The control group had a higher proportion of "primary behavior disorder" diagnoses than the treatment group (74% vs. 55%), whereas the treatment group had a higher proportion in the "psychoneurosis" category (28% vs. 20%). The authors argued that this difference favored the control group because the JBG clinics specialized in the treatment of primary behavior disorder. Others might suspect, however, that problems in the "psychoneurosis" category would be more likely to respond to treatment or to remit spontaneously than problems in the "primary behavior disorder" category and that the group difference may have favored the treatment group in the outcome comparison (see e.g., Barrett et al., 1978, pp. 416-417).

One year after the cases had been closed, they were followed up for an outcome assessment. The outcome for each child was classified as *success, partial success,* or *failure,* on the basis of assessments made by an evaluation committee that consisted of the JBG supervisor of casework, one of the agency psychiatrists, two psychiatric caseworkers, and a lay member of the agency board. Although some of these individuals would seem to have been closely involved in and knowledgeable about some of the cases, the report indicates that "the schedules were so prepared that the committee could not know whether the case being evaluated belonged in the Treatment or Control . . . groups" (Lehrman et al., 1949, p. 29). On the other hand, the material used by the committee in making evaluations was drawn from "social case records, including psychiatric and psychological reports, and from follow-up visits to the homes of the children" (p. 29); those who provided this raw material were employed by the agency being evaluated, and it seems likely that they knew or would have learned during the home visits whether the child had been treated or not.

At follow-up the percentage classified as *success* was significantly higher for treated than for control cases (50.5% vs. 31.8%); the percentage classified as *failure* was only slightly higher for control than for treated cases (30.0% vs. 26.0%). This pattern of results, the authors maintained, left "no doubt about the fact that the children in the JBG Treatment Group fared better in the community a year after closing than the children in the JBG Control Group" (Lehrman et al., 1949, p. 63). "The positive effect of the treatment," the authors maintained, "was established beyond a doubt" (p. 80).

In our view this verdict must be tempered somewhat by concerns about the diagnostic equivalence of the two groups and about the degree of "experimental blindness" and impartiality of those who provided the raw material used in evaluating outcomes. Nonetheless, the Lehrman et al. investigation stands as an important early methodological and substantive contribution to research on the outcome of clinic-based child mental health care.

The Levitt, Beiser, and Robertson (1959) study of clinic treatment.
The second study we will review within the treatment completer versus
dropout genre was conducted by Levitt et al. (1959). These investigators
focused on a sample of youngsters averaging about 10 years old when
first seen at the Institute for Juvenile Research, in Chicago; the sample
was 69% male. Levitt et al. compared outcomes for two groups: 237
treated cases, called "remainers," and 93 untreated cases, called "defectors." Defectors had been accepted for treatment but had dropped out
before the first therapy session. Those in the remainer group had had an
average of 18 therapy sessions, with therapy directed to the child alone
(10% of the cases), child plus parent (46%), or parent alone (44%).
Those who had received treatment elsewhere during the course of the
study were excluded from the sample. Remainer and defector groups
were compared on 61 clinical and background variables assessed at the
beginning of their clinic contact (e.g., gender, mental age, nature and
severity of problems). The groups were found to be quite similar; no
reliable group differences were found beyond chance expectancy
(Levitt, 1957a).[3]

Outcomes were assessed at an average of about 5 years after clinic
contact. The 26 outcome variables included scores on several psychological tests (e.g., Taylor Anxiety Scale, MMPI short form), parent and
child ratings (e.g., on current severity of original presenting problems),
clinician ratings (e.g., on manifest tension, affective tone of personality), and life adjustment indicators (e.g., completion of schooling,
institutional residence). Levitt et al. did not find remainer versus defector group differences on outcome measures beyond chance expectancy.
Examination of the *direction* of the group differences showed more
favorable scores for the defector group on 16, whereas only 9 of the
group differences favored the remainer group (sign test $p = .21$).

To enhance the possibility of identifying therapy effects, Levitt et al.
(1959) redefined the continuer group, requiring a minimum of 10
therapy sessions and reanalyzed for continuer-defector differences; the
results were essentially the same as in the original analyses, with no
reliable evidence that continuers were better adjusted at follow-up than
were defectors. Levitt et al. concluded that their findings "indicate that
there is no difference at follow-up between the adjustments made by
treated and untreated child patients" (1959, p. 345). In a discussion of
the study, Forstenzer (1959) described these no-difference findings as
so devastating that they constituted "an H-bomb."

The Ashcraft (1971) study of clinic treatment. More than a decade after Levitt et al. (1959), Ashcraft (1971) published another follow-up comparison of clinic-treated youngsters to matched children who had dropped out after intake and had remained untreated. All the youngsters in both groups had been seen initially at one of two participating clinics in a metropolitan area at some time during grades 3-6. The treatment group consisted of 40 children, 88% male, with a mean age of 9 years and 7 months, and a mean WISC IQ of 105.8. The dropout group numbered 43 and was 79% male, with a mean age of 9 years and 4 months, and a mean WISC IQ of 104.6. Ashcraft (1971) emphasized that "*all* children in the study were seen by the original diagnostic staff as emotionally disturbed and in need of treatment" (p. 339). On the other hand, the article provided no direct comparison of the two groups with respect to *degree* of disturbance or perceived need for treatment.

Ashcraft's (1971) outcome comparison of the two groups took place 5 years after the children's clinic contact. All the children in both groups had been classified as underachievers who had "learning difficulties" that "stemmed from emotional difficulties requiring outpatient treatment" (p. 339). Thus it may have been appropriate that Ashcraft assessed outcomes via measures of academic achievement. These measures consisted of changes over time in the Stanford Achievement Test Total Achievement Score, Total Language Achievement Score, and Total Quantitative Achievement Score. Although the measures seem conceptually appropriate, a critic might argue that achievement test scores may be relatively insensitive to therapy effects. Be that as it may, Ashcraft found no significant differences between treated and untreated children in total, quantitative, or language scores. When changes were compared from year to year over the follow-up period, the treated children appeared to improve over the first 2 years following therapy, then to decline over the next 3 years, such that their final scores were *below* those of the untreated children; no statistical tests were reported for these trends, however. Ashcraft noted that both treated and untreated children "continued to lag behind the normal school population each year for the five-year period. They did not reach the nine-month gain in achievement scores normally expected over the school year on the Stanford test for any of the five years" (1971, p. 340). Thus the Ashcraft study did not provide evidence that therapy was effective.

The Weisz and Weiss (1989) study of clinic treatment. The Levitt et al. (1959) study was conducted more than three decades ago, the Ashcraft (1971) study more than two. One might thus question whether the findings of these two studies are relevant to psychotherapy as it is currently practiced in clinics. To address this question, we now turn to a more recent study of clinic treatment in which we (Weisz & Weiss, 1989) compared treatment (continuer) and no-treatment (dropout) groups from nine outpatient mental health clinics. The continuer group consisted of 93 children who took part in at least 5 therapy sessions and who terminated with concurrence of their therapist; continuers averaged 12.4 sessions. The dropout group consisted of 60 children who had attended an intake session, who had been judged by the clinic staff to be in need of treatment, and who had been assigned a therapist but had not appeared for any sessions after intake. In addition, to ensure that the dropout group constituted a true no-treatment sample, we excluded from this group all who had received other mental health services during the period of the study. Continuers averaged 11.0 years of age (at the 6-month follow-up), and 64.5% were male; dropouts averaged 10.9 years of age, and 63.3% were male.

Comparability of the dropout and continuer groups was assessed by comparing the groups on variables that appeared potentially relevant to later outcomes. The variables included child demographic factors (age, gender, birth order), child clinical measures (CBCL internalizing, externalizing, and social competence scores; Child Depression Inventory scores, number of therapy sessions prior to this intake), and family factors (SES, number of children in the home, miles from home to clinic, and changes in family structure [e.g., separation or divorce, sibling moving away] during the 6 months following intake). Some 22 comparisons (11 at 6 months, 11 at 1 year) revealed no group differences beyond chance expectancy between the dropout and continuer groups.

At intake, 6 months later (after 98% of the children had completed treatment), and 1 year later (after all had completed treatment), we collected three measures of adjustment. CBCL (Achenbach & Edelbrock, 1983) parent reports were collected to provide information on a broad spectrum of clinically significant behavioral and emotional problems. Parents also gave severity ratings on up to three "major problems for which your child needs help" (identified at the time of intake); this assessment was intended to address specific problems that were a focus of treatment. Finally, Child Behavior Checklist Teacher Report Form (TRF; Achenbach & Edelbrock, 1986) teacher reports were collected to provide information on clinically significant behavioral and emotional problems from a source outside the family and not involved in the treatment process. (Teachers were asked to fill in the TRF as part of a "Youth Survey," and they were not told that the child had been to a clinic or had received treatment.)

At 6 months (for all dropouts and for all continuers who had completed treatment) and at 1 year, the two groups were compared on the three outcome measures described above, with intake scores covaried. On none of the three measures was a significant group difference found at 6 months or at 1 year. In other words, the findings revealed no reliable effect of clinic-based therapy on any of the measures.

To permit a rough comparison between these results and findings of the four meta-analyses of controlled studies, we calculated effect size (ES) estimates for the clinic data. Figure 5.1 presents these ES estimates. The 6-month CBCL assessment actually showed a trend toward worse outcomes for treated children than for dropouts; for all three measures at both points of assessment, ES estimates fell well below those found in the meta-analyses. Moreover, not one of the clinic treatment effect sizes was significantly different from 0.

Five possible explanations of the null results obtained for clinic treatment were examined by Weisz and Weiss (1989). These included the possibilities of (a) excessive variability in the data increasing the likelihood of null findings, (b) biased or defensive reporting by parents of dropout or continuer children, (c) hidden advantages favoring adjustment in the dropout group (e.g., the possibility that the dropout group was better adjusted than the treatment group at the time of intake), (d) immediate postintake improvement in the dropout group, which led to their dropping out, and (e) bias caused by the voluntary nature of subject participation in the research (e.g., the possibility that parents of dropouts who improved would be more likely to participate in the research than parents of dropouts who did not improve). The data and reasoning that could be brought to bear on these alternative explanations raised doubts about their plausibility (see Weisz & Weiss, 1989, pp. 745-746). In other words, examination of these alternative explanations did not appear to undermine the original finding that there had been no difference in outcome between treated and untreated groups.

One other point needs to be considered, a point relevant not only to the Weisz-Weiss study but also to all studies that use the treatment versus dropout comparison strategy to assess outcomes of therapy. Although these studies are not subject to some of the criticisms that

META FINDINGS   CLINIC FINDINGS

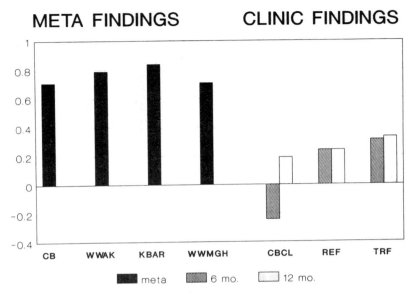

Figure 5.1. Effect Sizes Found in Four Meta-analyses of Child and Adolescent Psychotherapy Outcome Studies (CB = Casey & Berman [1985], WWAK = Weisz, Weiss, Alicke, & Klotz [1987], KBAR = Kazdin, Bass, Ayers, & Rodgers [1990; bar represents our estimate of the pooled ES, based on the Kazdin et al. report], WWMGH = Weisz, Weiss, Morton, Granger, & Han [1992; bar represents preliminary findings]), and in the clinic-based outcome study by Weisz & Weiss (1989; CBCL = Child Behavior Checklist findings, REF = findings on severity of primary referral problems, TRF = Teacher Report Form findings)

SOURCE: From "The Lab Versus the Clinic: Effects of Child and Adolescent Psychotherapy" by J. R. Weisz, B. Weiss, and G. R. Donenberg, in press, *American Psychologist.* Copyright © by the American Psychological Association. Reprinted by permission.

were directed at Levitt's (1957b) study, a potentially valid criticism is that clinic dropouts do not constitute a true "no-treatment" control group because the intake evaluation they receive may constitute a therapeutic intervention (see Barrett et al., 1978; Eisenberg & Gruenberg, 1961). It is also possible that the act of merely acknowledging that there is a problem for which help is needed may stimulate improved functioning and adaptation (see Hood-Williams, 1960). These points are useful and potentially important. However, if one pairs this argument with the data from the three most recent studies surveyed in this section, a logical inference might be that intake evaluation alone is about as effective as a full course of psychotherapy. Such an inference would certainly raise questions about the cost-effectiveness of the psychotherapy that takes place after intake.

A RANDOM ASSIGNMENT COMMUNITY-BASED STUDY: THE DE FRIES, JENKINS, AND WILLIAMS (1964) STUDY OF DISTURBED CHILDREN IN FOSTER CARE

Only 5 years after Levitt et al. (1959), De Fries et al. (1964) reported an unusual study involving a true procedural rarity in community-based treatment outcome research: *random assignment* to treatment versus control groups. The children sampled ranged in age from 6 through 15; all were described as seriously disturbed, and all had been assigned a psychiatric diagnosis. All were in foster care, and all had been selected from the caseload of the Department of Child Welfare of Westchester County, New York. From this pool, 27 pairs of children were formed, with members of each pair matched for age, gender, ethnic group, IQ, and psychiatric diagnosis. One member of each pair was selected randomly to receive the usual services of the welfare department; the other member of each pair received psychotherapy, together with enhanced social services for the foster family. After the pairs were formed but prior to intervention, three clinically experienced judges (who were blind to group assignment of the children) rated all the children on (a) relationships in the foster home, (b) adjustment in school and community, (c) symptomatology, and (d) well-being and productivity. Means on each of the four ratings were "almost identical" for the two groups, providing further evidence that the groups were closely matched.

Details of the intervention are sketchy in the published report. The therapy appears to have lasted 3 years and to have been conducted by professionally trained therapists who were supervised by a psychiatrist. The psychotherapy appears to have involved a mixture of "talk therapy" and play techniques aimed as such goals as verbalizing and acting out feelings and achieving a realistic self-image.

After the intervention, outside judges blind to group assignment were asked to use data from opening and closing psychiatric interviews to judge whether each child was *improved,* showed *no change,* or had *worsened* over time. The judges, working independently, agreed in 81% of their judgments and were in adjacent categories for the remaining

19%. Although the judgments were somewhat more favorable for the treated group than the control group, no significant treatment-control differences were found on this measure. In addition to the goal of achieving overall improvement in the children's adjustment, the investigators had hoped that the intervention would prevent children from being institutionalized. This goal was also not achieved, in that institutionalization occurred somewhat more often among the treated children than among those in the control group. In summary, this study, a rare example of random assignment methodology in a clinic/community setting, found no evidence of reliable treatment effects.

A TREATMENT "DOSAGE" APPROACH: THE WEISZ, WALTER, WEISS, FERNANDEZ, AND MIKOW (1990) STUDY OF YOUTH IN NORTH CAROLINA'S WILLIE M. PROGRAM

The final study we will review in this chapter involves an outcome assessment of not just psychotherapy in a clinic, but a broad-based community intervention program. The study also illustrates yet another approach to outcome assessment in the absence of randomly assigned control groups. The community intervention is North Carolina's Willie M. Program, named for one of the youngsters whose case stimulated the creation of the program. The program was established in 1981, following a class action suit on behalf of "seriously emotionally, neurologically, or mentally handicapped youth" who are "violent or assaultive" (North Carolina Department of Human Resources, 1989, p. 30). In the first 10 years of the program, about 2,800 violent and assaultive young people, most meeting traditional criteria as "delinquent youth," were certified as Willie M. class members; they received services averaging about $25,000 per person per year. The services included an array of community-based interventions ranging from outpatient psychotherapy and inpatient treatment to structured recreation programs and vocational training. In light of the array of services provided and the significant expense of the program ($250 million in the first 10 years), there was considerable interest in evaluating the intervention effects. Evaluation was hampered, however, by the absence of a true randomly assigned control group that had not received the services. In fact, because the program is legally mandated for all youth who meet the criteria for class membership, deliberately forming any no-treatment control group of Willie M. youth would be illegal in the state.

Given this situation, we had to find some naturally occurring comparison or control group within the legal constraints of the program. After considering several options, we settled on a comparison of two highly similar groups, both composed of individuals who had been certified as Willie M. class members during the early years of the program. Members of one group had all been certified class members for more than 1 year. This group had received services in the program for an average of 896 days; we called them the *long-certification* group. Members of the other group—the *short-certification* group—largely because their 18th birthdays fell near the time the program began, had been certified as class members so near their legally mandated "aging out" date that they had received little or no intervention through the program beyond the assignment of a case manager. The short group had averaged only 26 days of services in the program before aging out.

The long group included 147 people, the short group 21. The two groups were similar in ethnic and gender composition (long group = 19% female, short group = 25% female), in IQ (72.2 vs. 72.3), in age at first antisocial act (12.1 vs. 11.6), in *DSM-III-R* diagnostic profile, and even in the percentages from various regions of the state. There were very large differences, however, in intervention "dosage" received by the two groups. The long group had had much more of all the major categories of mental health intervention than had the short group (all $ps < .0001$).

We estimated the impact of the Willie M. Program on a measure that appeared directly relevant to the goals of the program: arrest after aging out. We carried out a survival analysis (Greenhouse, Stangle, & Bromberg, 1989; Miller, 1981) aimed at assessing whether individuals who had been in the Willie M. Program for a lengthy period and had received numerous services (i.e, the long-certification group) "survived" or remained unarrested longer than individuals in the short-certification group, following the termination of program services. Such a pattern would suggest that the Willie M. Program was effective in preventing behavior that leads to arrest; a failure to find this pattern, we reasoned, would cast some doubt on the efficacy of the program, at least with regard to this particular outcome.

Figure 5.2 presents the cumulative survival function for the long- and short-certification groups; this curve displays the proportion of each group surviving arrest, plotted as a function of the length of time since termination of Willie M. services. The curve for the short group is somewhat lower than the curve for the long group, indicating a somewhat higher arrest rate (i.e., a poorer survival rate) for the short-certification

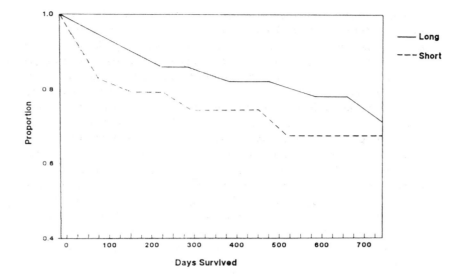

Figure 5.2. Arrest Survival Functions for Short-certification and Long-certification Groups of Former Willie M. Class Members

SOURCE: From "Arrests Among Emotionally Disturbed Violent and Assaultive Individuals Following Minimal Versus Lengthy Intervention Through North Carolina's Willie M. Program" by J. R. Weisz, B. R. Walter, B. Weiss, G. A. Fernandez, and V. A. Mikow, 1990, *Journal of Consulting and Clinical Psychology, 58,* 720-728. Copyright © 1990 by the American Psychological Association. Reprinted by permission.

group; however, the difference between groups did not approach statistical significance. We carried out a number of subsequent analyses to assess whether maximizing the advantage of the long-certification group in the comparison might generate a significant group difference. For example, we reran the comparison with a reconstituted long-certification group that included only those 69% of the cases judged by program staff to have had *all* their treatment and educational needs met and in the least restrictive setting possible. As another example, we reran the comparison with another reconstituted long-certification group that included only the 25% of the cases having the longest period of services in the program. None of the additional survival analyses showed a significantly better outcome for the long- than the short-certification group.

    We examined a number of possible artifactual explanations of our null findings. Could such findings have resulted from insufficient power in our design? A power test suggested that this was not the case. Could the no-difference finding have resulted from the fact that our follow-up period was limited to 2 years? This is possible, but it does not seem likely, given the fact that the 2-year period was sufficient to detect arrests in 29% of the sample. Might our failure to find outcome differences between short- and long-certification groups have obscured the possibility that both short and long periods of intervention had beneficial effects? This is conceivable; however, if a month or two of treatment proved to be as effective as more than 2 years of treatment, this would certainly raise questions about the cost-effectiveness of the *full-length* Willie M. Program (for a similar argument regarding more conventional psychotherapy, see above). Finally one might argue that arrest data are not the most sensitive index of program benefits and that measures of personality development or social functioning might be more likely to reveal positive effects. All these possibilities are worth considering. However, the fact remains that the data generated by this study do not support the efficacy of this large-scale community-based intervention with these disturbed, delinquent youth.

More broadly, reviews and meta-analyses of program evaluation research on interventions for delinquent youth over the past decade and a half have not reached very optimistic conclusions. Davidson, Gottschalk, Gensheimer, and Mayer (1984), for example, carried out a meta-analysis of 91 intervention studies with delinquent youth; they found that 60% of the studies showed some evidence of positive effects but that "when the actual size of the effects is considered . . . . there is no evidence that interventions with juvenile delinquents produce positive effects" (p. 28). This conclusion is similar to earlier assessments by Martinson (1974) and Greenberg (1977), who maintained "the blanket assertion that 'nothing works' is an exaggeration, but not by very much" (p. 141). Garrett (1985), in a meta-analysis of 111 intervention studies, found that treated delinquents functioned better, but only slightly, than untreated delinquents; and Whitehead and Lab (1989), in a meta-analysis of 50 post-1974 studies, had similar findings. Whitehead and Lab summarized their findings as follows: "The results show that interventions have little positive impact on recidivism and many appear to exacerbate the problem. . . . earlier evaluations that claim that 'nothing works' are close to the conclusion to be drawn from more recent evaluations of juvenile treatments" (1989, p. 276).

IMPLICATIONS OF THE CLINIC- AND
COMMUNITY-BASED FINDINGS

Taken together, the findings of the studies reviewed here stand in rather stark contrast to the meta-analytic findings reviewed in Chapters 3 and 4. With the exception of the Lehrman et al. (1949) report, the studies summarized in this chapter raise significant questions about the efficacy of some of the clinic-based psychotherapy and community-based mental health interventions used to address behavioral and emotional problems in young people. Certainly the methodologies used in these studies fall short of the pristine ideal, in that randomly assigned no-treatment control groups cannot be used in most cases. (For the one exception, see De Fries et al., 1964, reviewed above.) As we noted earlier, the conditions governing most clinic- and community-based intervention programs are not likely to permit the formation of such groups. On the other hand, the studies summarized in this chapter include several procedures designed to enhance the precision and meaningfulness of the comparisons made (e.g., documenting the demographic and clinical similarity of treated and untreated groups), and it would be imprudent to ignore the findings simply because randomly assigned control groups could not be formed in those cases. At the very least, the findings place a certain burden of proof on the research community: What we lack thus far is convincing evidence that the large positive effects of psychotherapy, demonstrated in controlled psychotherapy research and the meta-analyses thereof, are being replicated in the clinic and community settings where most real-life interventions actually occur.

SUMMARY

In this chapter we turned from experimental or "laboratory" studies of child therapy effects to outcome studies in clinic and community settings. We discussed the provocative reports by Eysenck (1952) on adult therapy and by Levitt (1957b) on child therapy, both comparing improvement rates in treated and untreated groups from different studies, and both finding no evidence that treatment was effective. Then we surveyed studies using more direct comparison procedures to assess therapy effects in clinic and community settings. One study (Shepherd et al., 1966) compared clinic-treated children to matched children from a general population survey. Four studies (Ashcraft, 1971; Lehrman et al., 1949; Levitt et al., 1959; Weisz & Weiss, 1989) compared clinic therapy dropouts to therapy completers. One study (De Fries et al., 1964) involved true random assignment of children in matched pairs to therapy versus no-therapy conditions. And one study (Weisz et al., 1990) involved a treatment "dosage" approach in which individuals receiving very little intervention were later compared to those who had received heavy doses of intervention. Only one of the studies reviewed (Lehrman et al., 1949) showed statistically significant effects of therapy; the remainder all had null findings. Although none of the studies is perfect methodologically, we argue that it would be a mistake to ignore this body of evidence. Taken together, the findings raise questions about whether the positive effects of child therapy that have been demonstrated in laboratory studies (the studies reviewed in Chapters 3 and 4) are generally replicated in service-oriented clinic and community settings.

NOTES

1. It is sometimes possible to assign children randomly to receive or not receive particular treatments in addition to the regular treatment program that all clinic children receive; what we refer to here are studies involving random assignment to standard clinic treatment versus no-treatment or active placebo conditions.

It is also sometimes possible to quasi-randomly assign clinic applicants to waiting-list control groups. This approach, however, has limitations that make it less than optimum empirically: (a) In most clinics, wait-list assignments cannot be truly random because children with particularly serious or pressing problems are likely to be moved to the front of the waiting list; (b) the wait-list procedure is only workable for short-term or time-limited therapy because withholding treatment for prolonged periods simply to match long-term therapy cases would violate the clinic mandate; and (c) for similar reasons the wait-list procedure is not likely to permit follow-up assessments because this would require withholding therapy from the wait-listed group for unacceptable periods of time.

2. We know of two other studies that approximate this methodology. However, both (Jacob, Magnussen, & Kemler, 1972; Witmer & Keller, 1942) have design features that make them not quite appropriate for inclusion here. Witmer and Keller (1942) reported no significant effects of therapy; Jacob et al. (1972) reported mixed findings.

3. The comparison of remainer and defector groups on clinical and background variables (Levitt, 1957a) appears to have been conducted on groups that overlapped with but were not identical to the remainers and defectors in the Levitt et al. (1959) treatment outcome study. The Levitt (1957a) study included 132 remainers and 208 defectors, whereas the Levitt et al. (1959) study included 237 remainers and 93 defectors.

6

SUMMING UP:
WHAT WE KNOW AND
WHAT WE NEED TO KNOW

In this final chapter, we will offer a broad overview of the picture painted by the previous chapters. In the process, we will address two questions: (a) From all the evidence reviewed in this book, what do we now know about the impact of child and adolescent psychotherapy? and (b) What do we need to know about therapy effects?

WHAT WE KNOW

The practice and study of psychotherapy with children and adolescents. In Chapter 1 we offered a broad survey of the practice and study of child psychotherapy. We noted that, over the course of a year, about 7.5 million American children and adolescents experience significant mental health problems for which they need help and that about a third of these receive some form of mental health treatment at a cost of about $1.5 billion. We discussed the kinds of problems that cause children to be referred to clinics (in the United States, most often undercontrolled problems) and the kinds of *DSM-III-R* diagnoses that are best represented among children in clinics (conduct/oppositional disorder is most often reported). We learned that 230 different forms of child therapy exist (see Kazdin, 1988), that most of these lack empirical evidence of efficacy, and that the three therapeutic models most often endorsed by practitioners are psychodynamic, behavioral, and cognitive. We characterized the literature on child and adolescent therapy as heavily theoretical and clinical-descriptive, complemented by a small but growing body of empirical studies of therapy and its impact. Finally we

90

discussed pros and cons of pooling the findings of such empirical studies via the technique known as meta-analysis; although we discussed several important criticisms of the technique, it was clear that several of the criticisms can be nullified by careful meta-analysts, and we concluded that the technique provides a fairer means of aggregating and summarizing findings from various studies than alternative methods such as the traditional narrative review.

Dropping out and staying in treatment. In Chapter 2 we addressed the question of who drops out and who stays in treatment. We noted that the question is important for at least two reasons: First, attrition from therapy is costly to clinics (which invest substantial clinic resources in beginning the process of therapy) and to children and their families (who lose the opportunity for professional help when they drop out); thus we need to understand as much as we can about which groups of children are at risk for dropping out. Second, youngsters who drop out are sometimes used as a naturally occurring control group in tests of the efficacy of clinic-based therapy (see Chapter 5); to establish the viability of this research strategy, we need to ensure that therapy dropouts are not different from therapy continuers at the beginning of their clinic contact in ways that might give the dropout group a superior prognosis. We reviewed 19 relevant studies, identified in a computer search. Focusing on demographic factors, child and parent clinical factors, and clinic factors, we found few significant differences between dropouts and continuers; the few that were significant were generally inconsistent in direction. The evidence was sufficient to warrant further exploration of a few possibilities—for example, that dropping out might be more likely among lower SES families than their higher SES counterparts. The few suggestive findings of this sort, however, generally pointed in the direction of a *worse* prognosis for dropouts than for treated children, and findings in this direction would support continued use of the "dropout comparison group" outcome research strategy as a conservative approach.

Correlates of psychotherapy effects. In Chapters 3 and 4 we sought to provide some evidence on the correlates of outcome in child and adolescent psychotherapy—for example, whether outcomes differed with different types of children or different types of therapy. Three of the meta-analyses (Casey & Berman, 1985; Weisz, Weiss, Alicke, & Klotz, 1987; Weisz, Weiss, Granger, Morton, & Han, 1992) provided several relevant tests, but the three did not examine exactly the same set of variables, and even where analyses matched, results often did not. We will touch on a few of the findings here.

Of special interest to us were findings bearing on the relative impact of different therapies. One of the most widely noted and widely bemoaned (see Parloff, 1984) findings of the Smith et al. (1980) meta-analysis of primarily adult outcome studies was that outcomes did not differ as a function of type of therapy. As Smith et al. (1980) put it, "Psychotherapy is beneficial, consistently so and in many ways. . . . Different types of psychotherapy (verbal or behavioral; psychodynamic, client-centered, or systematic desensitization) do not produce different types or degrees of benefit" (p. 184). In contrast to the Smith et al. observation, all four of the broad-based child meta-analyses discussed in Chapter 3 found significant ES differences as a function of therapy type, and so did the one specially focused meta-analysis in Chapter 4 that addressed this question. Kazdin, Bass, et al. (1990) found a mean ES of 0.59 for absolute differences between effects of contrasting treatments, although the specific treatments involved were not discussed in detail. Similarly, Hazelrigg et al. (1987) found that family therapy produced significantly higher effect sizes than alternative treatment approaches (again, not described in detail).

All three of the broad-based meta-analyses that specifically tested for behavioral versus nonbehavioral ES differences found that behavioral interventions produced larger ES values than nonbehavioral methods. However, when Casey and Berman (1985) eliminated all tests in which the outcome measures were similar to activities involved in the intervention, the behavioral versus nonbehavioral difference was apparently no longer significant (this is implied but not explicitly stated in their article). By contrast, in the two Weisz et al. (Weisz, Weiss, Alicke, & Klotz, 1987; Weisz, Weiss, Granger, Morton, & Han, 1992) meta-analyses, when tests involving outcome measures that were *unnecessarily* similar to intervention activities were removed, the superiority of behavioral over nonbehavioral methods remained significant. Moreover, in the two Weisz et al. meta-analyses, the superiority of behavioral therapy held up after eliminating tests were used to control for age of treated children, type of problem treated, and therapist training.

Both Casey and Berman (1985) and Weisz et al. (1992) found that therapy effects were positively correlated with the number of girls in the study sample. Weisz, Weiss, Alicke, and Klotz (1987) found that therapy effects were negatively correlated with age of the youngsters treated, but neither Casey and Berman (1985) nor Weisz et al. (1992) found such a relationship. Both of the Weisz et al. meta-analyses examined outcome as a function of therapist training (professional vs. student vs. paraprofessional); neither analysis found a main effect of this factor, but both found potentially important interactions with child age (see Chapter 3 for details on this and other findings). Among the numerous null findings, neither Casey and Berman (1985) nor Weisz et al. (1992) found a significant correlation between magnitude of ES and year of publication; this, of course, suggests the unhappy conclusion that neither our increased sophistication in outcome assessment nor our broadened array of therapeutic techniques has led to improvements over time in the efficacy of therapy. As we noted earlier, however, it is also possible that child therapy *is* more effective now than in the past but that journal editors are now more likely than before to accept outcome studies reporting null findings, so each trend offsets the other, and mean ES remains steady over time.

Overall effects of psychotherapy with children and adolescents: On the simple question, Does psychotherapy work? We turn now to a very broad and much-maligned question about therapy. In the literature on adult psychotherapy and on child and adolescent psychotherapy, it has become almost standard practice to cast aspersions on the question, Does psychotherapy work? The question is regarded by many writers as overly simplistic, too general, even passé. Research on psychotherapy outcomes, it is said, has now moved beyond that simple question to a more appropriately complex query: What form of psychotherapy, provided by whom, and under what conditions is most effective for which kinds of people, with what specific problems? (see Barrett et al., 1978; Bergin & Lambert, 1978; Kazdin, 1991; Paul, 1967).

Although we agree that this more focused form of the question has compelling value, we hasten to emphasize two key points about the simple question of overall efficacy. First, the overall question of whether psychotherapy is effective has value in its own right and should continue to be posed. As a parallel, consider the question, Does treatment of heart disease work? Cardiac researchers might argue that the question is much too simplistic—that is, that heart disease comes in many forms and to people of diverse physiology and risk status and that many different treatment regimens are available. This is all quite true, but despite this diversity—indeed, one could argue, *because of it*—the professional, research, and lay communities need periodic summary assessments of how we are doing overall in our efforts to treat heart disease. The same could be said of psychotherapy. Moreover, with the advent of meta-analysis, we have rather objective methods of providing such summary assessments. Second, the overall question of whether child and adolescent psychotherapy is effective cannot be dismissed as already having been answered. We should not assume that the general question is passé because the answer is already well known. On the contrary, the evidence reviewed in this book raises significant questions about what the fairest answer would be.

Research therapy versus clinic therapy: Does one effect size fit all? To elaborate, the evidence reviewed in the previous chapters suggests that the answer to the general question about therapy effectiveness may depend on what one considers to be the appropriate body of evidence. Two lines of evidence derived from two rather different research genres generate two rather different answers.

In the genre that might be called *research therapy,* interventions are conducted primarily for outcome evaluation purposes; in much of the therapy within this genre, youngsters are recruited for treatment rather than spontaneously referred, samples are selected for homogeneity (of treated problem and of other clinical and demographic characteristics), therapy addresses the focal problem(s) primarily or exclusively, therapists have recent and intensive training in the specific treatment methods that will be used, the therapy involves primary reliance on these specific methods, and the interventions are guided by treatment manuals and/or monitoring for treatment integrity.

In the other genre, which might be called *clinic therapy,* interventions are conducted for primarily clinical purposes, as part of an ongoing clinical service, and only occasionally are researchers able to examine the process and outcome. In much of the therapy within this genre, youngsters are clinic referred rather than recruited, samples cannot be selected for homogeneity, therapy addresses a relatively broad range of problems selected by the child and family (not by the therapist or clinic), therapists are not likely to have recent or intensive training in all the specific treatment methods needed, the therapy may well involve multiple methods, and the interventions are not likely to be guided by treatment manuals or systematic monitoring for treatment integrity.

When we surveyed the evidence from research therapy studies, as reflected in the four broad, general meta-analyses summarized in Chapter 3, we found a rather encouraging picture. The overwhelming majority of the studies in those meta-analyses showed significant positive effects of psychotherapy. The mean effect sizes identified in the different meta-analyses ranged from 0.71 to 0.84, averaging slightly below the 0.80 level classified as *large* by Cohen (1988). In every one of these meta-analyses, the average treated child scored better after therapy than at least three quarters of the control group children, averaging across the various outcome measures used. The evidence was also positive, though the ES values were lower, for the more focused meta-analyses of experimental therapy studies reviewed in Chapter 4. Those analyses revealed statistically significant beneficial effects of cognitive-behavioral methods and of family therapy, and one of the meta-analyses showed that various interventions generated positive changes in children's language performance. Thus the picture presented by the experimental studies within the research therapy genre was quite positive.

The findings with regard to clinic therapy studies were not nearly so positive. In Chapter 5 we reviewed the cross-study comparison by Levitt (1957b) and six additional studies within the clinic therapy genre. Only one of these seven articles (Lehrman et al., 1949) found that therapy had significant beneficial effects. That study focused on therapy conducted prior to April 1942, and it appears that the treated and untreated groups in that study may not have been well matched on the clinical conditions for which they were treated. Overall, the clinic therapy studies we have found reveal substantially more modest therapy effects than those identified in the research therapy studies; indeed the majority of the clinic therapy studies did not show significant effects.

The contrast between research therapy findings and clinic therapy findings can be viewed from several perspectives. We will note two of these here, and then we will return to this topic in the latter part of the chapter. On the one hand, it is possible to view the overall pattern of findings as quite encouraging. After all, the research therapy studies represent the best of our discipline, scientifically speaking. These studies show what substantial effects we can produce when we are able to maximize experimental control and procedural precision. Under such "laboratory" conditions, the evidence clearly indicates our experts in child psychotherapy have shown that child and adolescent interventions have measurable positive effects.

On the other hand, it is possible to find the overall pattern of results rather discouraging. The clinic therapy genre, one might argue, represents therapy as it is actually practiced, in real life, in service-oriented clinics that employ career clinicians. It is, after all, in such clinics where most of the 2.5 million youngsters who are treated in our country each year receive their treatment. If therapy works well in experimental labs but not in the settings where most troubled children and adolescents actually go for help, then we clearly have a problem. If studies of clinic therapy were to continue to replicate the null findings reported in Chapter 5, we might eventually face the risk of a kind of good news-bad news joke: The good news is that child psychotherapy works; the bad news is, not in real life. This risk necessitates some pondering on the second question posed at the beginning of this chapter: What do we need to know next about therapy effects?

WHAT WE NEED TO KNOW

How robust is the research therapy versus clinic therapy difference in outcomes? One of the most important questions we need to answer is whether the striking difference between outcomes of research therapy and clinic therapy as reported in this book is a reliable finding. Because the research therapy findings are already so well replicated (across more than 250 studies, with more than 15,000 subjects), much of the activity relevant to this question will necessarily focus on the replicability of the clinic therapy findings. It is important to recall that the clinic- and community-based studies reviewed here numbered only eight; only two were published within the past 5 years, with the other six having been published more than two decades ago, and three of those in the 1940s and 1950s. Thus the studies cannot be thought of as a representative sample of the psychotherapy conducted in the clinics of the 1990s. We need more current replications of these clinic- and community-based research procedures in order to generate evidence on therapy as it is *currently* practiced with children and adolescents.

Another limitation of the clinic- and community-based studies surveyed here is that they have emphasized services funded by the public and by charitable organizations, often for children and families with few or modest financial resources. We have little information on services provided through private practice clinics, employer-sponsored HMO programs, and the like. It is certainly possible that the resources of such service providers and of their more affluent clientele are associated with better treatment outcomes than those achieved by public clinics and services. Broadly put, what we need now are tests of the robustness of the clinic therapy findings across time, service, and setting.

What factor(s) account for the research therapy versus clinic therapy outcome difference? If these tests continue to show that research therapy is more effective than clinic therapy, we will need to know *why* such differences exist. Indeed, even if tests of robustness reveal circumstances in which outcomes are *not* attenuated in clinic settings, a major benefit of such a finding will be to help us understand why the outcome differences existed in the earlier studies. The range of possible explanatory factors is broad; here we will mention only a few.

One set of possibilities falls under the heading *artifactual explanations.* For example, clinic studies may have failed to generate statistically significant effects because of *low power,* due to such factors as small samples or highly variable outcome measures. The small sample explanation seems unlikely; the clinic studies generally used samples that were at least as large (and usually larger) than most lab studies. Limited statistical reporting makes it difficult to assess the possibility of unusually variable outcome measures, but those measures for which SDs are reported seem within the range of those used in the lab studies. Another possibility is that clinic studies use less careful measurement *procedures* than lab studies. Our methodological meta-analyses (Weiss & Weisz, 1990) did indicate that methodological precision is associated with increased ES, averaging across studies; this association, in turn, suggests that if clinic-based investigators were less careful procedurally than lab-based investigators, one result could be lower ES values for clinic therapy than for research therapy. These and other artifactual accounts of the findings may warrant study.

Another possibility is that the lab versus clinic outcome difference relates to *setting effects, therapist effects,* or the interplay of the two. Service-oriented clinics are busy places that often operate on inadequate budgets from state and local officials. As a result, the facilities may have a work-worn look, the staff may be under stress, and clients may not be greeted as warmly or treated as solicitously as are "subjects" in a research therapy study. In addition, the clinicians may be so overworked by paperwork, heavy caseloads, and clinic bureaucracy that their interactions with clients are affected adversely or their attention to the therapeutic task is undermined by factors for which neither they nor their clients are responsible. Clinician's caseloads and other work responsibilities may also mean that they have little time to stop and reflect on intervention plans for each client. And clinics may not have the resources needed to provide clinicians with regular updates and in-service training in specific clinical skills. By contrast, because the lifeblood of research therapy is treatable motivated subjects and well-trained therapists, research therapy investigators often do all that is within their power to ensure both.

Another possibility is that the lab versus clinic outcome difference results from *client effects.* The youngsters typically included in therapy experiments may represent a rather different population than those typically seen in clinics. Because research therapy studies so often rely on recruited subjects rather than true clinic-referred cases, it seems likely that the research subjects, on average, may be less disturbed than their clinic counterparts. It is also possible that the families who give consent for their children's participation in experiments may be higher in SES and lower in life stress, on average, than children who are treated in the publicly funded and charitably funded clinics where the clinic therapy studies have taken place.

Another possibility is that *therapy-type effects* may be involved. The Kazdin, Siegel, & Bass (1990) survey of 1,162 practicing psychologists and psychiatrists indicated that psychodynamic therapy, family therapy, and eclectic approaches were rated "useful most of the time, almost always, or always" (p. 191) more often than any other therapeutic approaches. These approaches were certainly well represented in the clinic therapy studies we reviewed in Chapter 5. By contrast, as Kazdin (1991) observed, "Psychodynamic, psychoanalytically oriented, family, and eclectic approaches [are] rarely studied" (p. 795) in experimental outcome research. The meta-analyses we reviewed in Chapters 3 and 4 certainly support this generalization; not one of the four categories mentioned by Kazdin (1991) and shown to be so popular among practicing clinicians (in Kazdin, Siegel, & Bass, 1990) was well represented in the pools of research therapy studies. This contrast between clinic and lab becomes potentially important when we recall the fact that behavioral approaches generated significantly larger effect sizes than nonbehavioral approaches in the meta-analyses (see above, and see Casey & Berman, 1985, for a possible exception). Thus it appears that the clinic therapy studies generally involve tests of nonbehavioral approaches, which have been shown to generate relatively modest effects, whereas the research therapy studies predominantly involve tests of behavioral and cognitive-behavioral approaches, which have been shown to generate substantial positive effects. It is possible, then, that this difference in therapeutic methods might alone account for much of the difference in outcome between clinic therapy and research therapy.

Precision and focus effects are also possible. In research therapy the therapist is apt to focus on a rather precisely defined problem or cluster of problems—say, aggression or "out-of-seat behavior"—and to devote most of the therapeutic effort to addressing that specific target. Moreover, as noted above, the intervention is apt to follow a well-developed treatment program designed specifically for the target problem and often detailed in a treatment manual and/or guided by close monitoring and supervision to ensure adherence to the treatment plan. By contrast, clinic therapy is much more likely to involve a rather heterogeneous array of problems, and this diffusion of focus may tend to dilute treatment efficacy with any particular problem. In addition, clinic therapy most often involves a treatment program that the therapist has to devise as he or she goes, no treatment manual, and relatively little external monitoring for adherence to a previously tested treatment program. This difference in focus and precision of the approaches may account for some of the difference in outcome between research therapy and clinic therapy.

A closely related possibility is that of *goodness-of-fit effects*. Stricker (1992) has envisioned "a movement toward developing specific prescriptive approaches for specific problems" (p. 545; see also Beutler & Clarkin, 1990). According to this vision, as therapists grow increasingly specialized in treating specific problems with sharply drawn techniques, "we practitioners will move from the current situation in which a patient may come in to our office and say 'I hope you treat what I have,' only to be told, 'I hope you have what I treat' " (Stricker, 1992, p. 545). In truth, research therapy approaches this vision even now. Most of what now constitutes the domain we have called *research therapy* involves rather precise fitting of specific problems to particular intervention techniques, such that young clients must "have what the therapist treats" in order to be included. By contrast, service-oriented clinics that serve the public can hardly be so discriminating. Indeed, to do so would likely be seen as violating the public trust and would certainly threaten the public support that all such clinics require for their very survival. As a consequence, the kinds of clinics represented in the clinic therapy studies generally treat an extremely broad array of youngsters and address an awesome array of problems, including some for which no demonstrably effective method of treatment has yet been developed. The fact that research therapists can pick and choose which children and which problems they will treat, maximizing goodness-of-fit between child problem and treatment technique, may give research therapy a distinct edge in the outcome comparison.

How are we to choose among all these competing explanations for the pattern of findings? Certainly our efforts will need to be guided by empirical work that has not yet been done. However, some already-completed empirical work may provide a point of departure. In Chapter 4 we reviewed the findings of Weiss and Weisz (1990) in which various aspects of design and methodology were examined for their impact on outcome study ES values. That study indicated that, at least in the meta-analytic sample of Weisz, Weiss, Alicke, and Klotz (1987), none of the following factors had a significant impact on ES: (a) clinic versus nonclinic setting, (b) clinic-referred versus nonclinic children, and (c) professional clinician versus nonprofessional therapist. These three findings cast at least some doubt on three of the explanations offered above for the superior effects of research therapy over clinic therapy. The findings of Weiss and Weisz may suggest by default that factors related to the types of therapy used, the precision and focus of therapeutic efforts, and the goodness of fit between child problem and treatment methods may all be promising foci for the next round of investigation.

We have reviewed here several perspectives on the ES difference between research therapy and clinic therapy studies. We have suggested that the difference may prove not to be very robust for public community clinics in the 1990s and that the difference may wash out if we assess clinic therapy as it takes place in private clinics. We have speculated about possible artifactual reasons for the clinic therapy versus research therapy outcome difference, and we have outlined several substantive single- and double-factor explanations that may account for much of the difference. Finally we reiterate that the clinic therapy studies conducted thus far fall short of the methodological ideal for outcome research, with random assignment of subjects to treatment and control conditions achieved in only one of the clinic studies we have found. Thus there is a clear need for careful replication and close evaluation of the findings with attention to the question of what they actually mean.

Although it would be a mistake to accept the clinic findings uncritically, it would also be a mistake to ignore or dismiss these findings and the serious state of affairs they define: At present, we do not have convincing evidence that the substantial positive effects of psychotherapy that have been demonstrated in controlled experimental research and underscored in the meta-analyses are being replicated in the clinic and community settings where most mental health interventions for children and adolescents actually occur.

WHERE TO GO FROM HERE:
AN AGENDA FOR THE NEXT GENERATION
OF RESEARCH

That rather unhappy summary statement brings us to a key question: Where do we go from here? A first step, outlined above, must certainly be replication of the outcome assessments in order to gauge the impact of clinic therapy in public and private clinics of the 1990s and beyond. Let us suppose, however, for the sake of discussion, that the clinic-based findings reported in Chapter 5 should be rather consistently replicated in modern clinics, such that the clinic therapy versus research therapy outcome difference noted in this book appears rather consistently. Let us further suppose that meta-analyses of the sort described in Chapters 3 and 4 continue to produce effect size values at least as strong as those reported in the two chapters. We would argue that such a state of affairs need not be viewed as entirely discouraging. Instead such findings might be likened to the proverbial glass that is both half-empty and half-full. From the half-empty point of view, clinic-based therapy for children may not be as effective as one would hope. But from the half-full point of view, the results of the meta-analyses suggest that, under proper conditions, child therapy may be quite effective. When the findings are cast in this light, a key task for researchers becomes that of identifying the "proper conditions" under which effects of child therapy may be maximized.

Finding conditions that maximize therapy effects. To identify those "maximizing" conditions that might actually make a difference in clinic settings, we may well need to adapt research therapies to actual clinical conditions with referred clients and then to test the efficacy of the research-based procedures in clinic settings. Over time, this process should help us properly interpret the kinds of findings reviewed in this book. As noted above, it is quite possible that research therapy has positive effects because, for instance, it tends to involve clear delineation of focal problems that will be targets of treatment (ruling out efforts to treat "the whole child"), precise matching of these problems to treatment methods, and/or selection of treatment methods that have empirical support. On the other hand, as we also noted above, it is possible that research therapy appears more effective, in part, because the youngsters being treated are less seriously disturbed or are more responsive to intervention than those youngsters typically treated in clinics or because research therapists are free of constraining conditions (e.g., heavy caseloads) under which clinic therapists often work. Until we bring the various elements of research therapy into the clinics and test their impact in these service-oriented settings, it will be difficult to evaluate the various interpretive possibilities in a definitive way, and it may also be difficult to point the way to enhanced therapy outcomes in clinics.

   Renewing ties between research and practice. Constructing research that brings research therapy into the clinic will almost certainly require enriched collaboration between researchers and clinical practitioners, and this process is apt to be healthy for both groups. It has certainly been one of the most frequently voiced complaints of practicing clinicians over the years that psychotherapy research is of little value to them (see Elliott, 1983; Kupfersmid, 1988; Luborsky, 1972; Orlinsky & Howard, 1978; Parloff, 1980). As Strupp (1989) stated it, psychotherapists "have recurrently complained that they can learn but little from psychotherapy research" (p. 717). It is particularly telling that, when clinical psychologists are asked to rank order the usefulness of various sources of information to their practice, research articles and books are generally placed at the bottom of the scale (Cohen, 1979; Cohen, Sargent, & Sechrest, 1986; Morrow-Bradley & Elliott, 1986). A number of researchers have voiced concerns about the clinical relevance of their work; as Morrow-Bradley and Elliott (1986) note, "With virtual unanimity, psychotherapy researchers have argued that (a) psychotherapy research should yield information useful to practicing therapists, (b) such research to date has not done so, and (c) this problem should be remedied" (p. 188).

   In our view one of the overall messages of this book is that psychotherapy research with children may have considerable relevance to the work of clinicians and, conversely, that the work of clinicians is very relevant to research. If it is true that child therapy is more effective under research conditions than under clinic conditions, outcome research may well prove useful to practicing clinicians and their young clients by specifying those conditions under which therapeutic gains can be secured and maximized. On the other hand, to achieve this goal, researchers will need to draw from a reservoir they all too rarely tap: the wisdom and perspective of clinicians whose knowledge about children and treatment has been shaped in the crucible of real life.

REFERENCES

Achenbach, T. M., & Edelbrock, C. S. (1983). *Manual for the Child Behavior Checklist and Revised Child Behavior Profile.* Burlington: University of Vermont, Department of Psychiatry.

Achenbach, T. M., & Edelbrock, C. S. (1986). *Manual for the Teacher's Report Form.* Burlington: University of Vermont, Department of Psychiatry.

American Psychiatric Association. (1987). *Diagnostic and statistical manual of mental disorders* (3rd ed., rev.). Washington, DC: Author.

Appelbaum, M. I., & Cramer, E. M. (1974). Some problems in the nonorthogonal analysis of variance. *Psychological Bulletin, 81,* 335-343.

Ashcraft, C. W. (1971). The later school adjustment of treated and untreated emotionally handicapped children. *Journal of School Psychology, 9,* 338-342.

Baekeland, F., & Lundwall, L. (1975). Dropping out of treatment: A critical review. *Psychological Bulletin, 82,* 738-783.

Baker, L., & Cantwell, D. P. (1987). Comparison of well, emotionally disordered and behaviorally disordered children with linguistic problems. *Journal of the American Academy of Child Psychiatry, 26,* 193-196.

Barrett, C. L., Hampe, I. E., & Miller, M. C. (1978). Research on child psychotherapy. In S. L. Garfield & A. E. Bergin (Eds.), *Handbook of psychotherapy and behavior change: An empirical analysis* (2nd ed., pp. 411-435). New York: John Wiley.

Barrnett, R. J., Docherty, J. P., & Frommelt, G. M. (1991). A review of child psychotherapy research since 1963. *Journal of the American Academy of Child and Adolescent Psychiatry, 30,* 1-14.

Beitchman, J., & Dielman, T. (1983). Terminators and remainers in child psychiatry: The patient-treatment fit. *Journal of Clinical Psychiatry, 44,* 413-416.

Bergin, A. E., & Lambert, M. J. (1978). The evaluation of therapeutic outcomes. In S. L. Garfield & A. E. Bergin (Eds.), *Handbook of psychotherapy and behavior change: An empirical analysis* (pp. 139-189). New York: John Wiley.

Beutler, L. E., & Clarkin, J. (1990). *Systematic treatment selection: Toward prescriptive psychological treatment.* New York: Brunner/Mazel.

Bonner, B. L., & Everett, F. L. (1986). Influences of client preparation and problem severity on attitudes and expectations in child psychotherapy. *Professional Psychology, Research and Practice, 17,* 223-229.

Bornstein, B. (1949). Analysis of a phobic child. *Psychoanalytic Study of the Child, 3-4,* 181-226.

Casey, R. J., & Berman, J. S. (1985). The outcome of psychotherapy with children. *Psychological Bulletin, 98,* 388-400.

Cohen, J. (1988). *Statistical power analyses for the behavioral sciences* (2nd ed.). Hillsdale, NJ: Lawrence Erlbaum.

Cohen, J. C., Davine, M., & Meloche-Kelly, M. (1989). Prevalence of unsuspected language disorders in a child psychiatric population. *American Academy of Child and Adolescent Psychiatry, 28,* 107-111.

Cohen, L. (1979). The research readership and information source reliance of clinical psychologists. *Professional Psychology, 10,* 780-785.

Cohen, L., Sargent, M., & Sechrest, L. (1986). Use of psychotherapy research by professional psychologists. *American Psychologist, 41,* 198-206.

Cohen, R. L., & Richardson, C. H. (1970). A retrospective study of case attrition in a child psychiatric clinic. *Social Psychiatry, 5,* 77-83.

Cole, J. K., & Magnussen, M. G. (1967). Family situation factors related to remainers and terminators of treatment. *Psychotherapy: Theory, Research, and Practice, 4,* 107-109.

Cottrell, D., Hill, P., Walk, D., Dearnaley, J., & Ierotheou, A. (1988). Factors influencing non-attendance at child psychiatry out-patient appointments. *British Journal of Psychiatry, 152,* 201-204.

Davidson, W. S., Gottschalk, R., Gensheimer, L., & Mayer, J. (1984, May). *Interventions with juvenile delinquents: A meta-analysis of treatment efficacy.* Paper presented at the Joint NIMH/NIJ Conference on Crime and Substance Abuse, Washington, DC.

De Fries, Z., Jenkins, S., & Williams, E. C. (1964). Treatment of disturbed children in foster care. *American Journal of Orthopsychiatry, 34,* 615-624.

DeWitt, K. (1978). The effectiveness of family therapy: A review of outcome research. *Archives of General Psychiatry, 35,* 549-561.

Durlak, J. A., Fuhrman, T., & Lampman, C. (1991). Effectiveness of cognitive-behavior therapy for maladapting children: A meta-analysis. *Psychological Bulletin, 110,* 204-214.

Eiduson, B. T. (1968). Retreat from help. *American Journal of Orthopsychiatry, 38,* 910-921.

Eisenberg, L., & Gruenberg, E. M. (1961). The current status of secondary prevention in child psychiatry. *American Journal of Orthopsychiatry, 31,* 355-367.

Elliott, R. (1983). Fitting process research to the practicing psychotherapist. *Psychotherapy: Theory, Research, and Practice, 20,* 47-55.

Ewalt, P. L., Cohen, M., & Harmatz, J. S. (1972). Prediction of treatment acceptance by child guidance clinic applicants: An easily applied instrument. *American Journal of Orthopsychiatry, 42,* 857-864.

Eysenck, H. J. (1952). The effects of psychotherapy: An evaluation. *Journal of Consulting Psychology, 16,* 319-324.

Eysenck, H. J. (1978). An exercise in mega-silliness. *American Psychologist, 33,* 517.

Feldman, E. (1938). Why children discontinue child guidance treatment. *Smith College Studies in Social Work, 9,* 27-98.

Forstenzer, H. M. (1959). Discussion. *American Journal of Orthopsychiatry, 29,* 347-349.

Gaines, T. (1978). Factors influencing failure to show for a family evaluation. *International Journal of Family Counseling, 6,* 57-61.

Gaines, T., & Stedman, J. M. (1981). Factors associated with dropping out of child and family treatment. *American Journal of Family Therapy, 9,* 45-51.

Garrett, C. J. (1985). Effects of residential treatment on adjudicated delinquents: A meta-analysis. *Journal of Research in Crime and Delinquency, 22,* 287-308.

Glass, G. V., & Kliegl, R. M. (1983). An apology for research integration in the study of psychotherapy. *Journal of Consulting and Clinical Psychology, 51,* 28-41.

Glass, G. V., McGaw, B., & Smith, M. L. (1981). *Meta-analysis in social research.* Beverly Hills, CA: Sage.

Golden, L. (1944). Why clients of a child guidance clinic fail to return after the initial interview. *Smith College Studies in Social Work, 15,* 128-129.

Gould, M. S., Shaffer, D., & Kaplan, D. (1985). The characteristics of dropouts from a child psychiatry clinic. *Journal of the American Academy of Child Psychiatry, 24,* 316-328.

Greenberg, D. F. (1977). The correctional effects of corrections: A survey of evaluations. In D. A. Greenberg (Ed.), *Corrections and punishment* (pp. 95-158). Beverly Hills, CA: Sage.

Greenfield, J. (1972). *A child called Noah.* New York: Holt, Rinehart & Winston.

Greenfield, J. (1978). *A place for Noah.* New York: Holt, Rinehart & Winston.

Greenhouse, J. B., Stangl, D., & Bromberg, J. (1989). An introduction to survival analysis: Statistical methods for analysis of clinical trial data. *Journal of Consulting and Clinical Psychology, 57,* 536-544.

Greenwald, S., & Russell, R. L. (1991). Assessing rationales for inclusiveness in meta-analytic samples. *Psychotherapy Research, 1,* 1-8.

Gurman, A. S., Kniskern, D. P., & Pinsof, W. M. (1986). Research on the process and outcome of marital and family therapy. In S. L. Garfield & A. E. Bergin (Eds.), *Handbook of psychotherapy and behavior change* (pp. 565-624). New York: John Wiley.

Halpern, W. I. (1968). Do children benefit from psychotherapy? A review of the literature on follow-up studies. *Bulletin of the Rochester Mental Health Center, 1,* 4-12.

Hazelrigg, M. D., Cooper, H. M., & Borduin, C. M. (1987). Evaluating the effectiveness of family therapies: An integrative review and analysis. *Psychological Bulletin, 101,* 428-442.

Hedges, L. V. (1982). Estimation of effect size from a series of independent experiments. *Psychological Bulletin, 92,* 490-499.

Hedges, L. V., & Olkin, I. (1985). *Statistical methods for meta-analysis.* New York: Academic Press.

Heinicke, C. M., & Goldman, A. (1960). Research on psychotherapy with children: A review and suggestions for further study. *American Journal of Orthopsychiatry, 30,* 483-494.

Hood-Williams, J. (1960). The results of psychotherapy with children: A reevaluation. *Journal of Consulting and Clinical Psychology, 24,* 84-88.

Hunt, R. G. (1962). Occupational status and the disposition of cases in a child guidance clinic. *International Journal of Social Psychiatry, 8,* 199-210.

Institute of Medicine (IOM). (1989). *Research on children and adolescents with mental, behavioral, and developmental disorders.* Washington, DC: National Academy Press.

Jacob, T., Magnussen, M. G., & Kemler, W. M. (1972). A follow-up of treatment terminators and remainers with short-term and long-term symptom duration. *Psychotherapy: Theory, Research, and Practice, 9,* 139-142.

Karpe, M. (1942). Resistance and anxiety as factors in the discontinuance of child guidance treatment. *Smith College Studies in Social Work, 12,* 374-414.

Kazdin, A. E. (1978). Evaluating the generality of findings in analogue therapy research. *Journal of Consulting and Clinical Psychology, 46,* 673-686.

Kazdin, A. E. (1982). *Single-case research designs: Methods for clinical and applied settings.* New York: Oxford University Press.

Kazdin, A. E. (1983). Meta-analysis of psychotherapy: Criteria for selecting investigations. *Behavioral and Brain Sciences, 8,* 296.

Kazdin, A. E. (1985). The role of meta-analysis in the evaluation of psychotherapy. *Clinical Psychology Review, 5,* 35-47.

Kazdin, A. E. (1988). *Child psychotherapy: Developing and identifying effective treatments.* Elmsford, NY: Pergammon.

Kazdin, A. E. (1990). Premature termination from treatment among children referred for antisocial behavior. *Journal of Child Psychology and Psychiatry, 31,* 415-425.

Kazdin, A. E. (1991). Effectiveness of psychotherapy with children and adolescents. *Journal of Consulting and Clinical Psychology, 59,* 785-798.

Kazdin, A. E., Bass, D., Ayers, W. A., & Rodgers, A. (1990). Empirical and clinical focus of child and adolescent psychotherapy research. *Journal of Consulting and Clinical Psychology, 58,* 729-740.

Kazdin, A. E., Bass, D., Siegel, T., & Thomas, C. (1989). Cognitive-behavioral therapy and relationship therapy in the treatment of children referred for antisocial behavior. *Journal of Consulting and Clinical Psychology, 57,* 522-535.

Kazdin, A. E., Siegel, T. C., & Bass, D. (1990). Drawing on clinical practice to inform research on child and adolescent psychotherapy: Survey of practitioners. *Professional Psychology: Research and Practice, 21,* 189-198.

Kendall, P. C. (1981). Cognitive-behavioral interventions with children. In B. B. Lahey & A. E. Kazdin (Eds.), *Advances in clinical child psychology* (Vol. 4, pp. 53-90). New York: Plenum.

Kupfersmid, J. (1988). Improving what is published: A model in search of an editor. *American Psychologist, 43,* 635-642.

Lake, M., & Levinger, G. (1960). Continuance beyond application interviews at a child guidance clinic. *Social Casework, 41,* 303-309.

Lefebvre, A., Sommerauer, J., Cohen, N., Waldron, S., & Perry, I. (1983). Where did all the "no-shows" go? *Canadian Journal of Psychiatry, 28,* 387- 390.

Lehrman, L. J., Sirluck, H., Black, B. J., & Glick, S. J. (1949). *Success and failure of treatment of children in the child guidance clinics of the Jewish Board of Guardians, New York City* (Jewish Board of Guardians Research Monographs, No. 1). New York: Jewish Board of Guardians.

Lessing, E. E., Black, M., Barbera, L., & Seibert, F. (1976). Dimensions of adolescent psychopathology and their prognostic significance for treatment outcome. *Genetic Psychology Monographs, 93,* 155-168.

Levitt, E. E. (1957a). A comparison of "remainers" and "defectors" among child clinic patients. *Journal of Consulting Psychology, 21,* 316.

Levitt, E. E. (1957b). The results of psychotherapy with children: An evaluation. *Journal of Consulting Psychology, 21,* 189-196.

Levitt, E. E. (1958). A comparative judgmental study of "defection" from treatment at a child guidance clinic. *Journal of Clinical Psychology, 14,* 429-432.

Levitt, E. E. (1971). Research on psychotherapy with children. In A. E. Bergin & S. Garfield (Eds.), *Handbook of psychotherapy and behavior change* (pp. 474-493). New York: John Wiley.

Levitt, E. E., Beiser, H. R., & Robertson, R. E. (1959). A follow-up evaluation of cases treated at a community child guidance clinic. *American Journal of Orthopsychiatry, 29,* 337-347.

Lowman, R. L., DeLange, W. H., Roberts, T. K., & Brady, C. P. (1984). Users and "teasers": Failure to follow through with initial mental health service inquiries in a child and family treatment center. *Journal of Community Psychology, 12,* 253-262.

Luborsky, L. (1972). Research cannot yet influence clinical practice. In A. Bergin & H. H. Strupp (Eds.), *Changing frontiers in the science of psychotherapy* (pp. 120-127). Hawthorne, NY: Aldine.

Magder, D., & Werry, J. S. (1966). Defection from a treatment waiting list in a child psychiatric clinic. *Journal of the American Academy of Child Psychiatry, 5,* 706-720.

Manderscheid, R. W., & Sonnenschein, M. A. (Eds.). (1990). *Mental health, United States, 1980.* Rockville, MD: National Institute of Mental Health.

Mann, C. (1990). Meta-analysis in the breech. *Science, 249,* 476-480.

Martinson, R. (1974). What works? Questions and answers about prison reform. *Public Interest, 10,* 22-54.

McAdoo, W. G., & Roeske, N. A. (1973). A comparison of defectors and continuers in a child guidance clinic. *Journal of Consulting and Clinical Psychology, 40,* 328-334.

McGuire, J., Bates, G. W., Dretzke, B. J., McGivern, J. E., Rembold, K. L., Seabold, D. R., Turpin, B. M., & Levin, J. R. (1985). Methodological quality as a component of meta-analysis. *Educational Psychologist, 20,* 1-5.

Michelson, L. (1981). Psychotherapeutic outcome for children in a community mental health center: Psychological, demographic, and treatment predictors. *Psychological Reports, 48,* 323-326.

Milazzo-Sayre, L., Benson, P. R., Rosenstein, M. J., & Manderscheid, R. W. (1986). *Use of inpatient psychiatric services by children and youth under age 18, United States, 1980.* Rockville, MD: National Institute of Mental Health.

Miller, R. G. (1981). *Survival analysis.* New York: John Wiley.

Mintz, J. (1983). Integrating research evidence: A commentary on meta-analysis. *Journal of Consulting and Clinical Psychology, 46,* 71-75.

Morris, D. P., & Soroker, E. P. (1953). A follow-up study of a guidance clinic waiting list. *Mental Hygiene, 37,* 84-88.

Morrow-Bradley, C., & Elliott, R. (1986). Utilization of psychotherapy research by practicing psychotherapists. *American Psychologist, 41,* 188-197.

Neter, J., & Wasserman, W. (1974). *Applied linear statistical models.* Homewood, IL: Irwin.

North Carolina Department of Human Resources. (1989). *Report to the governor and the general assembly on the Willie M. Program, 1988-1989.* Raleigh: Author.

Novick, J. (1980). Negative therapeutic motivation and negative therapeutic alliance. *Psychoanalytic Study of the Child, 35,* 299-320.

Novick, J., Benson, R., & Rembar, J. (1981). Patterns of termination in an outpatient clinic for children and adolescents. *Journal of the American Academy of Child Psychiatry, 20,* 834-844.

Office of Technology Assessment (OTA). (1986). *Children's mental health: Problems and services—A background paper* (Publication No. OTA-BP-H-33). Washington, DC: Government Printing Office.

Orlinsky, D., & Howard, K. (1978). The relation of process to outcome in psychotherapy. In S. Garfield & A. Bergin (Eds.), *Handbook of psychotherapy and behavior change: An empirical analysis* (2nd ed., pp. 283-330). New York: John Wiley.

Parloff, M. B. (1980). Psychotherapy and research: An anaclitic depression. *Psychiatry, 43,* 279-293.

Parloff, M. B. (1984). Psychotherapy research and its incredible credibility crisis. *Clinical Psychology Review, 4,* 95-109.

Paul, G. L. (1967). Outcome research in psychotherapy. *Journal of Consulting Psychology, 31,* 109-118.

Pekarik, G., & Stephenson, L. A. (1988). Adult and child client differences in therapy dropout research. *Journal of Clinical Psychology, 17,* 316-321.

Persons, J. B. (1991). Psychotherapy outcome studies do not accurately represent current models of psychotherapy: A proposed remedy. *American Psychologist, 46,* 99-106.

Plunkett, J. W. (1984). Parents' treatment expectations and attrition from a child psychiatric service. *Journal of Clinical Psychology, 40,* 372-377.

Prioleau, L., Murdock, M., & Brody, N. (1983). An analysis of psychotherapy versus placebo studies. *Behavioral and Brain Sciences, 6,* 275-310.

Raudenbush, W. W., Becker, B. J., & Kalaian, H. (1988). Modeling multivariate effect sizes. *Psychological Bulletin, 103,* 111-120.

Richman, L. C., & Lindgren, S. D. (1981). Verbal mediation deficits: Relation to behavior and achievement in children. *Journal of Abnormal Psychology, 90,* 99-104.

Rosenthal, R. (1979). The "file drawer problem" and tolerance for null results. *Psychological Bulletin, 86,* 1165-1168.

Rosenzweig, S. (1954). A transvaluation of psychotherapy—A reply to Hans Eysenck. *Journal of Abnormal Psychology, 49,* 298-304.

Ross, A. O., & Lacey, H. M. (1961). Characteristics of terminators and remainers in child guidance treatment. *Journal of Consulting Psychology, 25,* 420-424.

Russell, C., Olson, D., Sprenkle, D., & Atilano, R. (1983). From family symptom to family system: Review of family therapy research. *American Journal of Family Therapy, 11,* 3-14.

Russell, R. L., Greenwald, S., & Shirk, S. R. (1991). Language change in child psychotherapy: A meta-analytic review. *Journal of Consulting and Clinical Psychology, 59,* 916-919.

Saxe, L., Cross, T., & Silverman, N. (1988). Children's mental health: The gap between what we know and what we do. *American Psychologist, 43,* 800-807.

Schubert, D., & Miller, S. (1981). Social class and perceived improvement in therapy: The effects of therapist discipline and therapy type. *Hillside Journal of Clinical Psychiatry, 3,* 71-80.

Shapiro, D. A., & Shapiro, D. (1982). Meta-analysis of comparative therapy outcome studies: A replication and refinement. *Psychological Bulletin, 92,* 581-604.

Shapiro, D. A., & Shapiro, D. (1983). Comparative therapy outcome research: Methodological implications of meta-analysis. *Journal of Consulting and Clinical Psychology, 51,* 42-53.

Shepherd, M., Oppenheim, A. N., & Mitchell, S. (1966). Childhood behavior disorders and the child-guidance clinic: An epidemiological study. *Journal of Child Psychology and Psychiatry, 7,* 39-52.

Singh, H., Janes, C. L., & Schechtman, J. M. (1982). Problem children's treatment attrition and parents' perception of the diagnostic evaluation. *Journal of Psychiatric Treatment Evaluation, 4,* 257-263.

Sirles, E. A. (1990). Dropout from intake, diagnostics, and treatment. *Community Mental Health Journal, 26,* 345-360.

Sledge, W. H., Benarroche, C. L., & Phillips, S. H. (1988). Adolescent elopement from a psychiatric hospital: Multiple dimensions. *Journal of Nervous and Mental Disease, 176,* 562-567.

Smith, M. L., & Glass, G. V. (1977). Meta-analysis of psychotherapy outcome studies. *American Psychologist, 32,* 752-760.

Smith, M. L., Glass, G. V., & Miller, T. L. (1980). *Benefits of psychotherapy.* Baltimore: Johns Hopkins University Press.

Stark, K. D., Reynolds, W. M., & Kaslow, N. J. (1987). A comparison of the relative efficacy of self-control therapy and a behavioral problem-solving therapy for depression in children. *Journal of Abnormal Child Psychology, 15,* 91-113.

Stricker, G. (1992). The relationship of research to clinical practice. *American Psychologist, 47,* 543-549.

Strube, M. J., Gardner, W., & Hartmann, D. P. (1985). Limitations, liabilities, and obstacles in reviews of the literature: The current status of meta-analysis. *Clinical Psychology Review, 5,* 63-78.

Strube, M. J., & Hartmann, D. P. (1983). Meta-analysis: Techniques, applications, and functions. *Journal of Consulting and Clinical Psychology, 51,* 14-27.

Strupp, H. H. (1989). Psychotherapy: Can the practitioner learn from the researcher? *American Psychologist, 44,* 717-724.

Tuma, J. M. (1989). Mental health services for children. *American Psychologist, 44,* 188-199.

Tuma, J. M., & Pratt, J. M. (1982). Clinical child psychology practice and training: A survey. *Journal of Clinical Child Psychology, 11,* 27-34.

Ulrici, D. (1983). The effects of behavioral and family interventions on juvenile recidivism. *Family Therapy, 10,* 25-36.

Viale-Val, G., Rosenthal, R. H., Curtiss, G., & Marohn, R. C. (1984). Dropout from adolescent psychotherapy: A preliminary study. *Journal of the American Academy of Child Psychiatry, 23,* 562-568.

Weiss, B., & Weisz, J. R. (1990). The impact of methodological factors on child psychotherapy outcome research: A meta-analysis for researchers. *Journal of Abnormal Child Psychology, 18,* 639-670.

Weisz, J. R. (1986). Contingency and control beliefs as predictors of psychotherapy outcomes among children and adolescents. *Journal of Consulting and Clinical Psychology, 54,* 789-795.

Weisz, J. R., Suwanlert, S., Chaiyasit, W., & Walter, B. R. (1987). Over- and undercontrolled referral problems among children and adolescents from Thailand and the United States: The *wat* and *wai* of cultural differences. *Journal of Consulting and Clinical Psychology, 55,* 719-726.

Weisz, J. R., Walter, B. R., Weiss, B., Fernandez, G. A., & Mikow, V. A. (1990). Arrests among emotionally disturbed violent and assaultive individuals following minimal versus lengthy intervention through North Carolina's Willie M. Program. *Journal of Consulting and Clinical Psychology, 58,* 720-728.

Weisz, J. R., & Weiss, B. (1989). Assessing the effects of clinic-based psychotherapy with children and adolescents. *Journal of Consulting and Clinical Psychology, 57,* 741-746.

Weisz, J. R., & Weiss, B. (1991). Studying the "referability" of child clinical problems. *Journal of Consulting and Clinical Psychology, 59,* 266-273.

Weisz, J. R., Weiss, B., Alicke, M. D., & Klotz, M. L. (1987). Effectiveness of psychotherapy with children and adolescents: A meta-analysis for clinicians. *Journal of Consulting and Clinical Psychology, 55,* 542-549.

Weisz, J. R., Weiss, B., & Donenberg, G. R. (in press). The lab versus the clinic: Effects of child and adolescent psychotherapy. *American Psychologist.*

Weisz, J. R., Weiss, B., & Langmeyer, D. B. (1987). Giving up on child psychotherapy: Who drops out? *Journal of Consulting and Clinical Psychology, 55,* 916-918.

Weisz, J. R., Weiss, B., & Langmeyer, D. B. (1989). On "dropouts" and "refusers" in child psychotherapy: Reply to Garfield. *Journal of Consulting and Clinical Psychology, 57,* 170-171.

Weisz, J. R., Weiss, B., Morton, T., Granger, D., & Han, S. (1992). *Meta-analysis of psychotherapy outcome research with children and adolescents.* Unpublished manuscript, University of California, Los Angeles.

Wells, R., & Dezen, A. (1978). The results of family therapy revisited: The nonbehavioral methods. *Family Process, 17,* 251-273.

White, D. M., Rusch, F. R., Kazdin, A. E., & Hartmann, D. P. (1989). Applications of meta-analysis in individual-subject research. *Behavioral Assessment, 11,* 281-296.

Whitehead, J. T., & Lab, S. P. (1989). A meta-analysis of juvenile correctional treatment. *Journal of Research in Crime and Delinquency, 26,* 276-295.

Williams, R., & Pollack, R. H. (1964). Some nonpsychological variables in therapy defection in a child-guidance clinic. *Journal of Psychology, 58,* 145-155.

Wilson, G. T. (1985). Limitations of meta-analysis in the evaluation of the effects of psychological therapy. *Clinical Psychology Review, 5,* 35-47.

Wilson, G. T., & Rachman, S. J. (1983). Meta-analysis and the evaluation of psychotherapy outcome: Limitations and liabilities. *Journal of Consulting and Clinical Psychology, 51,* 54-64.

Witmer, H. L., & Keller, J. (1942). Outgrowing childhood problems: A study in the value of child guidance treatment. *Smith College Studies in Social Work, 13,* 74-90.

INDEX

ABOUT THE AUTHORS

John R. Weisz is Professor of Psychology and Director of the Doctoral Program in Clinical Psychology at the University of California, Los Angeles. He received his BA in Psychology from Mississippi College in 1967. After three years as a Peace Corps volunteer in Kenya, he studied at Yale University where he received his MS and his PhD. He has held faculty positions at Cornell University, the University of North Carolina at Chapel Hill, and the Medical College of Virginia where he also served as Director of Psychology and Research at the Virginia Treatment Center for Children. His primary research interests lie in the areas of child and adolescent psychopathology and psychotherapy.

Bahr Weiss is Assistant Professor in the Clinical Psychology Training Program at Peabody College of Vanderbilt University. He received his PhD from the University of North Carolina at Chapel Hill. His current research interests include the effectiveness of child psychotherapy under naturalistic conditions, developmental differences in the expression of depression, the relation between aggression and depression in children, and quantitative analysis.